AF604481

Jerome Doraisamy is a lawyer from Sydney, New South Wales. He attended St Aloysius' College and then the University of Technology, Sydney, where he graduated with a Bachelor of Laws and Bachelor of Arts in Communication (Social Inquiry). Over the course of his legal career he has worked in a range of fields, from commercial practice to academic research to a major federal government inquiry. *The Wellness Doctrines* is his first book.

www.thewellnessdoctrines.com

hello@thewellnessdoctrines.com

The WELLNESS DOCTRINES

for Law Students & Young Lawyers

Jerome Doraisamy

Foreword by Sir Gerard Brennan AC KBE GBS

in consultation with Dr Robert Fisher MBBS FRANZCP

10% of proceeds from the sales of The Wellness Doctrines will be donated to the Tristan Jepson Memorial Foundation. The Foundation's objective is to decrease work related psychological ill-health in the legal community and to promote workplace psychological health and safety. Legal organisations across Australia can become signatories to the Foundation's Best Practice Guidelines, which assist members of the profession to understand the initiatives and methods of management that assist in the creation and maintenance of psychologically healthy and supportive workplaces. Go to www.tjmf.org.au to find out more about the work of the Foundation.

First published by Jerome Doraisamy in 2015 in association with Xoum
Reprinted in 2015 (twice), 2016, 2022

Reprinted in 2022 by:
Booktopia Publishing, a division of Booktopia Group Ltd
Unit E1, 3-29 Birnie Avenue, Lidcombe, NSW 2141, Australia

ISBN 978-1-921134-95-1 (print)
ISBN 978-1-921134-96-8 (digital)

All rights reserved. Without limiting the rights under copyright below, no part of this publication shall be reproduced, stored in or introduced into a retrieval system, or transmitted in any form or by any means (electronic, mechanical, photocopying, recording or otherwise), without the prior permission of both the copyright holder and the publisher.

The moral right of the author has been asserted.

Text copyright © Jerome Doraisamy 2015
Illustrations copyright © Sam Moore 2015
Author photograph copyright © Nikki To 2015
Internal design and typesetting copyright © Xoum Publishing 2015

Cataloguing-in-publication data is available from the National Library of Australia

Cover design by Sam Moore and Xou Creative (Brio Books), briobooks.com.au
Printed and bound in Australia by Pegasus Media & Logistics

The paper in this book is FSC® certified. FSC® promotes environmentally responsible, socially beneficial and economically viable management of the world's forests.

Testimonials

"My only regret in seeing *The Wellness Doctrines* is that I did not see it earlier. For various reasons, most of them touched on in this book, depression has been my constant (but unwelcome) companion in life. People attracted to study law probably do so (at least in part) because they are attracted to standing up for what is right: fighting for justice is a very attractive prospect. But the idealism we have at law school can look out of place in the shiny offices of a big law firm, and many young lawyers find themselves engaged in complex, tiring work which seems to have no connection at all with justice. Many, including the brightest and best, see their earlier ideals looking more naïve; more unachievable. More undergraduate. It is depressing to see that you have exhausted yourself building a bridge over the wrong river. Or a bridge that falls down. Or a bridge, when you really meant to build a skyscraper. Law is a demanding activity. It does not often allow much space for reflection and adjustment. It does not grant leave to pause and ask: Is this what I had in mind when I enrolled in law school? But striving for justice is as worthwhile now as when you enrolled. If enough young lawyers have the courage to say 'I'm depressed, I need help' they will make a more effective generation of lawyers."

Julian Burnside (Australian barrister and human rights advocate)

"Jerome Doraisamy deserves the appreciation of all law students and junior lawyers for his considerable contribution to the discussion about mental wellbeing in the study and practice of the law. His new book provides very helpful and practical guidance to law students and young lawyers on how to safeguard and care for their mental health. The book also helps to remove the stigma concerning mental health issues. It encourages those suffering from anxiety, depression and/or bipolar disorder to seek early help. It carries the very important 'you are not alone message' and emphasises that no matter how badly one may feel affected by poor mental health, there will always be someone else who has travelled the same journey and understands your predicament completely. Jerome's book also provides extremely helpful insights into how to discern signs of mental distress in others and to help them on their journey to mental wellness. The book comes at an important time when law student associations, law societies and bar associations are seeking to put emphasis on assisting their members as the profession comes to acknowledge the severe problem confronting it if it fails to properly address and act on the challenges which impact the mental health of its members."

Justice Shane Marshall (Judge, Federal Court of Australia)

"This is an insightful and practical guide addressing a vital issue for our time. The personal stories will both encourage and warn."

The Hon. Keith Mason, AC QC (former President, NSW Court of Appeal)

"In spite of the fact that mental illness is so common, living with illnesses such as depression is an isolating and confusing experience. *The Wellness Doctrines*, with its powerful personal stories interspersed with good clinical information and practical strategies to manage stressful situations, will help break down the isolation and confusion. This valuable new resource will hopefully also be read by friends, colleagues and managers, so that legal workplaces become non-stigmatising, supportive and productive environments for everyone."

Barbara Hocking (former Executive Director, SANE Australia)

"An extremely important book that needed to be written...one that should be required reading for all law students and everyone involved in the legal profession. While *The Wellness Doctrines* is focused on the legal profession, it contains a universal message and for this reason is applicable to all students set to embark upon highly demanding careers, and those currently working in highly demanding careers."

Danny Baker (*Huffington Post* Health and Wellness blogger; author, *I Will Not Kill Myself, Olivia* and *Depression is a Liar*)

"The student and graduate voice is critical in the success of the movement to address the high levels of psychological distress that we know Australian law students are experiencing. As the founder of the Wellness Network for Law I am heartened by the contribution to this movement that *The Wellness Doctrines* makes. Drawing on his own experience, and the lived experience of many other legal professionals and students, Jerome takes a positive and empowering approach to the serious issue of law student and lawyer mental wellbeing by highlighting possible solutions, strategies and practical tools that can combat the prevalence, causes and effects of mental ill-health and support success and wellness in the law."

Dr Rachael Field (Coordinator, Australian Wellness for

Law Network; Associate Professor in Law at Queensland University of Technology)

"An open and honest account of personal stories and experiences within the legal profession, *The Wellness Doctrines* will aid in the ongoing positive changes that are occurring in the legal fraternity so that everyone addresses their mental wellbeing as well as to support those with mental health issues. Jerome has done a great job pulling together stories, statistics and, most importantly, practical advice for those who may find themselves dealing with mental health challenges. *The Wellness Doctrines*, while targeted at law graduates and students, provides some guiding tools and tips that would be beneficial for any young professional heading into a competitive and challenging work environment."

Sebastian Robertson (Founder and Director, Batyr)

"Levels of depression and suicide in the legal profession are unacceptably high. Understanding why this occurs, destigmatising the issue and ensuring people get the right help at the right time are critical to turning this around. By sharing the stories and opinions of those within the profession this book will shine a light on this important issue and help many struggling alone."

Jonathan Nicholas (CEO, ReachOut Australia)

"I applaud that a book is being written to support young lawyers and shed light on the challenges faced by them in contemporary society. It is a profession which is close to my heart and I congratulate Jerome for being brave. Thank you for writing such an honest account and for raising awareness on an important topic we need to discuss."

Tamara Cannon (Founder and CEO, Lille Fro)

"A refreshing and enjoyable book to read. Like a lot of other students, I have juggled considerable interests away from studies throughout my degree and knew the stress that deadlines and pressure can bring. I appreciate the practical solutions that Jerome provides and above all the honesty of his experience."

Pat McCabe (retired Australian rugby union player "Wallaby #847"; current law student)

"In this honest and empowering book, Jerome Doraisamy breaks down stigma and offers practical advice for overcoming one of the most significant issues faced by law students and legal professionals."

Kathryn Crossley (Editor and co-founder, *Survive Law*)

"*The Wellness Doctrines* is a must-have tool for every law student and young lawyer. This book not only grapples with the broader issues such as the stigma attached to mental ill-health – thereby encouraging an important discussion on this topic – but it also provides incredibly useful and practical tips and strategies that all law students and young lawyers would benefit in applying to their own lives and daily routines. With an increasingly upward trend in the number of young students and lawyers facing a range of mental health issues, we are grateful to the author for his hard work in taking proactive steps to address this worrying problem and encourage those suffering to seek help and support. We also applaud all those who took the brave step in coming forward to talk about their experiences: their stories, as featured in this book, will undoubtedly change the lives of many law students and young lawyers for the better."

The Australian Law Students' Association, 2014–15 Executive

Disclaimer

The Wellness Doctrines is a practical self-help guide which addresses the subjects and issues pertaining to depression in law. The book is not meant to be, nor should it be, used as a substitute for consultation, diagnosis or treatment by a medical professional. It offers anecdotes and experiences of law students and lawyers who have provided peer feedback, as well as strategies and solutions for young legal professionals that have been discussed with mental health experts.

The opinions expressed by the author and those providing comments or opinions are theirs alone. These views are not intended to be truthful factual representations and the author is not responsible for the accuracy of any of the information supplied by those people who been interviewed and/or whose comments appear in this book. Except where specifically stated, the author does not endorse the statements and opinions of those quoted in this book. Where interviewees have requested that their identity remain anonymous a pseudonym has been used. Any resemblance to, or reflection of, actual people who bear those names is entirely coincidental and the opinions attributed to the anonymous interviewees should not be attributed to those actual people.

References to health resources are provided for informational purposes only and do not constitute endorsement of such resources over other existing outlets unless otherwise specified. The information was correct at the time of printing. Readers should be aware that contact details for some resources might have changed following the publication of this book.

Contents

Testimonials v
Disclaimer xi
Author's Note xvii
Expert's Note xx
Foreword xxi

Jerome's Story, Part I: What went wrong? 1
Legal Profession vs. Depression: **Jerome's case for change** 8
Signs and symptoms of depression in law 11
Why is there such a stigma about depression in law? 17
Should I be fearful of my chosen profession? 19
TWD Wellbeing Wisdom 25
I don't have depression. Why should I worry? 27
The importance of being proactive 29
TWD Wellbeing Wisdom 35
If law can be bad for your health, why do it? 37
What can the study and practice of law give you? 39
TWD Wellbeing Wisdom 46
Personalities, Part I: Identifying our legal idiosyncrasies . . 48
Pessimism 49
Perfectionism and competitiveness 52
So where do we go from here? 57
Personalities, Part II: Overcoming our legal idiosyncrasies 58
Learn to be okay with not always being number one. 59
Direct your attention elsewhere, when need be 60
Have outside activities that inspire you 60

Manage the expectations of the environment that you are in 61
Calm down 62
Have helpful, practical mentors 63
Focus on the things you can control, not the things you can't 64
Learn to ask questions and seek help, rather than going at it alone 64
Chat regularly with your friends. 65
Have connections outside of law that provide different perspectives 66
Focus on the client, not the politics 67
TWD Wellbeing Wisdom 69

How can law teachings and practices affect our wellbeing? 71

Adopt a refocused approach on students' thought processes . . . 74
Overly demanding assessments in law school. 76
Is legal work too negatively geared? 77
Allow yourself personal space and time. 79
Law does not have to be your life – so don't let it take over . . . 79
Internal influences on the legal environment. 81
Perceived lack of autonomy 83
Law vs. The Rest of The World 85
TWD Wellbeing Wisdom 86

The importance of individual responsibility 88

What it means to look after yourself. 91
TWD Wellbeing Wisdom 98

What works and doesn't work when managing your health and wellbeing? 100

What *does* work? 101
What *doesn't* work?. 105
TWD Wellbeing Wisdom 108

It's so hard to find a job in law. What can I do? 111

Manoeuvring and managing the job market 112
Extrapolate your skills and interests 114
Control what you can 116
TWD Wellbeing Wisdom 119

Choosing the right job for me 120
Learning how to pick the perfect career 122
TWD Wellbeing Wisdom 129
How can I manage an often onerous workload in law? . . 131
Prioritise other things in your life. 132
Practise efficiency and discipline. 134
Exercise transparency and open communication 135
Set achievable goals 136
Choose the right cultural fit for you 137
Set time limits – be strategic and avoid perfectionism 139
TWD Wellbeing Wisdom 142
How can I unwind when I'm stressed at my desk? 143
Stepping outside the office 145
Listening to music 147
Mindfulness and meditation 147
Social endeavours. 149
Preparedness and organisation 150
A cup of tea 151
TWD Wellbeing Wisdom 153
What is the best way for me to achieve a work/life balance? 156
Socialising 158
Volunteering 159
Sports and outdoor activities 160
Academic endeavours. 161
Finding time for yourself 162
What if I give up an existing hobby? 163
TWD Wellbeing Wisdom 165
I already have a busy schedule. If I take on a hobby, won't I become even more tired and stressed? 166
How to manage your timetable and combat wellbeing issues 167
TWD Wellbeing Wisdom 173
Do we have a tendency to self-medicate with alcohol? . . 175
What effect does drinking have upon our wellbeing? 178
TWD Wellbeing Wisdom 185

What have other people experienced? How do I know I'm not alone? 187

What have our TWD Champions experienced? 189

What have our TWD Champions witnessed in others? 190

TWD Wellbeing Wisdom 193

How can I help my friends, colleagues or classmates who have such health issues? 195

What are the ways to show support to those around me? 196

TWD Wellbeing Wisdom 204

What makes law such an important profession in our society, and how can I help effect meaningful change? . . 206

The importance of law in our society 208

How lawyers can effect meaningful change 210

TWD Wellbeing Wisdom 212

Resources: I need help. What can I do, where can I go, who can I turn to? 215

Websites/blogs 217

Organisations and networks 219

Charities and depression hotlines 221

Initiatives founded by lawyers 223

TWD Wellbeing Wisdom 225

Jerome's Story, Part II: Where am I now? 226

Acknowledgements 229

Select bibliography 233

Author's Note

Dr Robert Fisher, Head of The Department of Psychiatry and Psychological Services at St Vincent's Clinic and Private Hospital, reports the following about persons suffering from mental illness:

> *"When people have been severely depressed, they talk about the physical and psychological pain that they experience. They report being profoundly unhappy, lacking energy, drive and motivation, not being able to sleep, being highly agitated or anxious. They may contemplate suicide and feel very isolated, as though no one really understands what they're going through. They often feel that they're a burden on others and that everyone would be better off, including themselves, if they were dead."*

The legal profession experiences alarmingly high rates of psychological distress, anxiety and depression – higher than in most (if not all) other professions.

Unfortunately, I was one of them.

This self-help "survival guide" showcases a bounty of experiences and anecdotes as a means to highlight the many solutions and strategies that can be undertaken – by lawyers, with lawyers and for lawyers. Ultimately, the aspiration is that you will be armed with the practical tools necessary to become the best legal professional that you can be.

Recorded interviews were conducted with three expert individuals and institutions, as well as 45 legal professionals from across the board: current law students, law graduates and young solicitors, managing partners, academics, deans and a former commissioner of a national legal body. These interviewees shared their own experiences, what they witnessed in their friends and colleagues, and what they think can be done to improve the culture of law, so that the legal profession can retain a sense of duty to society: to serve the community in the most just, efficient and productive manner possible. This can only be achieved if a lawyer takes a holistic approach to the study and practice of law. Such an approach can be best accomplished if one recognises the need for such proactivity from an early point in their legal career.

Not all interviewees had experienced health issues themselves; rather, they were encouraged to provide a broader perspective into how said issues can and do affect their friends and colleagues, and subsequently the legal profession as a whole. Some of them are named, others opted for anonymity (and thus have pseudonyms). Regardless of whether or not an interviewee has their name attributed to their quotes, I am grateful to all of them; they showed great courage in speaking with me.

Symptoms of depression can affect any person, regardless of profession, but unfortunately it is extremely prevalent in law. If you are suffering from depression, you are not alone. There is help for you. You can become the legal professional you want and were meant to be. Use this guide as a handy resource. It may be beneficial to you in more ways than one.

The Wellness Doctrines is dedicated to every future law student and young lawyer entering or practising in the legal field. Depression can have devastating and incapacitating effects on your self-confidence, career success and personal life; these are issues that should not be wished upon anyone. Ten per cent of all proceeds generated from this book will be donated to the Tristan Jepson Memorial Foundation. As Tristan's 2004 suicide highlighted, one lawyer suffering from depression is one too many.

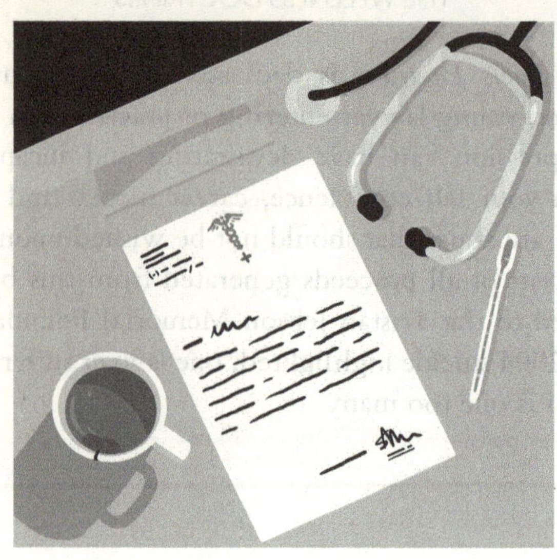

Expert's Note Dr Robert Fisher, MBBS FRANZCP

Dr Robert Fisher is the Head of The Department of Psychiatry and Psychological Services at St Vincent's Clinic and Private Hospital, and a board member for the Tristan Jepson Memorial Foundation.

Jerome's book is an important contribution to tackling the most common and most disabling mental illnesses affecting lawyers, from students to judges. It is so good to see members of the profession taking responsibility for self-care and care for their colleagues. Perhaps this is a reflection of a wish to re-emphasise that law is still an honourable profession, not just a business. It shows what can be achieved when groups of people act in a civilised, intelligent way to care for and bring out the best in their community.

Foreword Sir Gerard Brennan, AC KBE GBS

Sir Gerard Brennan, AC KBE GBS, served as the tenth Chief Justice of the High Court of Australia. He was appointed to this position – the highest-ranking judicial office in the Commonwealth – in 1995 by the then Prime Minister, The Hon. Paul Keating. Sir Gerard served a total of 17 years on the High Court (1981–1998), the last three of which were served as Chief Justice. During his tenure, he was the presiding justice in the High Court's now famous Mabo *decision.*

This is a book of its time and it is a book for its time. It is a book of its time because it reveals the stresses that nowadays beset entrants into the legal profession in this country. The pathways of entry have changed during my professional lifetime. In the post WWII years, the law schools of the Australian universities, then comparatively few in number, drew their undergraduates from school leavers and from an older and more mature cohort of returned servicemen. Many were full-time students. There were very few women students. Not all aspiring lawyers chose to obtain their qualification for admission by studying at a university; many were admitted on satisfying the requirements specified by the respective professional associations of barristers and solicitors. Academic success was valued but admission to study and employment as a recent graduate did not evoke the intense academic competition that now seems to mark the pathway into professional qualification.

The present demography of the younger legal profession and of aspirants to legal qualifications reveals a different picture. Today, undergraduates fill the lecture halls of our proliferating law schools, competing for access to the universities, for academic success there and for employment in the practising profession. Jerome Doraisamy has lived through, and describes in this book, the problems that are the consequence of this competitive demand. The stimuli for this demand are various; they combine to place significant pressure on those seeking admission to undergraduate law courses and, later, on those applying for employment or commencing a legal practice. I suspect that a majority of today's undergraduates are engaged simultaneously in study and in some form of paid employment, leaving them short of time and subject to serious levels of stress. And, as the proportion of undergraduates to those already in the practising profession has blown out, employment prospects have correspondingly diminished. The pressure to achieve, in study and in employment, places great pressure on the student and the young lawyer.

The risk of depression brought on by these or other factors is very real, and Jerome has frankly, and therefore authoritatively, identified many of the risks in this book. His own experience in dealing with his depression and his candid acknowledgement of that experience inspired his research for and writing of this book. It is a tribute to his altruism that, even after he dealt with the problems which beset him, he persisted in getting together the materials needed to ensure that the book would offer practical and safe assistance to others who might find themselves at risk.

This is a book for its time because, having charted the factors which might precipitate the onset of depression in an undergraduate or young lawyer, it offers practical suggestions about preventing the illness or combating it. A reader who may have some concern about his or her own wellbeing may find Jerome's identification of the danger signs to be a helpful assurance that others have travelled the same path and have emerged healthy and happy after frankly addressing the problem. In identifying the danger signs and in suggesting preventive or remedial steps, Jerome has not been restricted to his own experience. He has drawn widely on the experience of others and liberally quotes others' statements of that experience. He believes that law students and young lawyers possess the idiosyncrasies of pessimism, perfectionism and competitiveness. These attitudes, if uncontrolled, are a danger to health and wellbeing. But they need not do damage. There are countervailing factors. The study of law and its practical operation can be inspirational because a lawyer becomes aware that assisting to maintain the rule of law is a vital service given to the community. This inspiration, Jerome asserts, is "a means to overcome psychological distress, depression and/or anxiety". But he does not assume that high ideals are sufficient by themselves. He offers practical, workaday suggestions, tested by him and by others, to safeguard mental health. However, he does not claim to be qualified in psychiatry. He suggests canons of behaviour to eliminate depression and to return the student or young lawyer to health and happiness, but he submits his suggestions to professional review by Dr Robert Fisher. Perhaps central to Jerome's message is the need for "law students and young lawyers to take control and responsibility for their own mental health", conscious of the reality that they are not alone and that it is both normal and wise to ask for help.

This is an optimistic book for it tells the story of a person who, after spending time in the slough of despond, took responsibility for his own mental health, sought help and was restored to health and happiness. That is a timely message directed to aspiring and practising lawyers who are aware of the risks to mental health involved in coping with the intense pressures of their calling. It is a message of hope and confidence.

Jerome's Story, Part I: What went wrong?

It was the evening of Thursday 29 December 2011 and I was at the Falls Festival in Lorne, Victoria, with a group of school friends. We had arrived a few hours earlier, set up our campsite, had our pre-drinks, and were gearing up for the first night of what promised to be a raucous, hair-raising week of New Year partying. It was a trip that I had been looking forward to for a number of months. I was so glad that it had finally arrived.

However, once I finally arrived at the festival, I found myself struggling to get into the swing of things; I just wasn't feeling as excited as my friends clearly were, nor was I projecting an outward sense of enthusiasm. I couldn't quite put my finger on it, so I deduced that I was still stressed and frazzled from the past year and hadn't had a chance to properly let my hair down. Unfortunately, in a few short hours, I realised in brutal fashion that I was wrong and that wasn't the case.

My friends and I were perched in one of the big-top tents listening to our first band of the festival. I was comfortably tipsy at this point and my friends were charging towards ill-cautioned inebriation. But I still wasn't having any fun. It was frustrating me...I had been eagerly anticipating this holiday for months. And I had achieved everything that I wanted to and more in the previous calendar year, including widespread recognition for my work on-campus for law students at UTS. In addition, I was halfway through a summer clerkship with a leading commercial law firm. I was now at a famous music festival in the beautiful country of southern Australia with my best friends.

On paper, everything was going exactly how I would have wanted it to. And then it hit me...I wasn't having fun because I wasn't happy.

I found myself overcome by waves of emotions, one after the other, all crashing down on me before I'd had adequate time to absorb and process the previous one. I wasn't happy. I had pushed myself so hard the past 24 months that I simply had no energy left to expend – nothing else to give. Truthfully, I was so deeply consumed by my stress, anxiety and expectations that I had rendered myself utterly incapable of functioning on what any reasonable person would perceive to be a normal level. In fact, I was so far removed from my friends' lives that I couldn't properly relate to them in a social environment or converse with my family about personal matters. I was so emotionally and psychologically detached from the reality that everyone else seemed to exist in, that I didn't realise, until that very moment, just how much trouble I was in.

If we had been anywhere other than a very visible public

place, I may have very well screamed right then and there. Instead, I sobbed silently – fighting with every ounce of strength not to cry in front of my friends, all of whom were absorbed in their own exuberance: dancing, singing and, most significantly to me, though through no fault of their own, oblivious to my state.

Somehow, I managed to make it through the night. Internally I was ripping myself to pieces, but outwardly I projected composure; I forced smiles and kept my friends company. Why, I thought, should I burden them with my troubles? They had paid good money to attend the festival, and there was no way I was going to be selfish and dampen their spirits with my own problems. I had an obligation to be a dutiful friend and ensure that everyone was having a good time…even if it meant I was utterly miserable and alone with my tumult.

By morning, and after a sleepless night, I knew I had to go home. I pulled aside my two best friends, Angus and Michael, and told them in no uncertain terms that I believed that I had depression, had likely been encumbered with it for a while, and needed to head back to Sydney immediately to manage my affairs, before I did any more damage to myself, or even those around me. They listened intently and put up no fight. They agreed that I should do what I felt was best for me and helped me leave the festival so I could make the journey home. Not only that, they pulled it off in a manner that didn't draw attention to my departure from the group. Honestly, I wasn't sure how I would respond if someone asked me why I was leaving, so I was grateful that I didn't have to.

As I journeyed home, the one thought that kept returning was, how on Earth did this happen to me? What the hell went wrong?

The best way I can explain the circumstances that led to my breakdown is to give an outline of my schedule at that time: 2011 – I was undertaking a double degree in law and communications, on a full-time study schedule at the University of Technology, Sydney (UTS), working as a paralegal at a law firm two or three days a week, and volunteering approximately 30–35 hours a week for the UTS Law Students' Society (LSS) as its Vice President. In 2010 I had much the same schedule, with the only difference being that I volunteered fewer hours for the UTS LSS, in exchange for being Assistant Producer for the UTS Law Revue. I also participated in additional extracurricular activities such as writing articles for law journals and working for public sector charities and organisations on the weekends. And all of this occurred before I could even attend to my personal and social life. This was an extraordinary workload for a guy in his early twenties to take on. Frankly, it would have been a huge schedule for even the most seasoned professional. Without a doubt I had been experiencing a relatively high level of anxiety in regards to the professional world and my place in it. This was also compounded by a lifelong shyness and insecurity, along with an intense personal desire to perform.

So the events of the past three years were by no means the only contributing factors. But if I had not ventured down the path that I did, I may have never experienced a breakdown, which means you would have never had the opportunity to read this book.

I'm not sure exactly when it happened, but at some point in those first few days I resolved to be proactive and critically analytical about my situation. For me, this entailed being upfront and honest with my family and friends, and doing whatever necessary to get better as soon as possible. I then commenced tackling the situation with a black and white approach. That is, I believed that, if I created a mental "to do" list of the things I needed to do to get better, then I would in fact get better. My focus on the health and wellbeing of law students at UTS while I was Vice President led me to deduce that, if I followed certain steps, I would be okay. Paradoxically, this ultimately worsened matters. In fact, ticking off mental health tasks not only didn't make me feel better; it actually exacerbated my frustration, thereby making me feel worse.

The next year, 2012, was, without argument, the toughest and most emotionally draining year of my life. Crying became a release that was so important to me that I sometimes secretly scheduled time during the day to just "let go".

In October of that year – in the same week that I graduated from university and was admitted as a solicitor in New South Wales – I voluntarily checked myself into the Northside Clinic in Cremorne on Sydney's North Shore. I told almost nobody about my hospitalisation – not even my parents or siblings, who were abroad at the time. In fact, the only people who knew were my two roommates, Codie and Jack, and my ex-girlfriend. Staying in the hospital was something that I would never have visualised for myself, but at that point it seemed like the smartest and frankly safest thing to do. The feeling of security that I received from just being there, and away from home, was beneficial in itself. That entire period of my life is something I recall as an out-of-body experience, in the sense that it is hard to fathom or appreciate just how fragile I was. It's a state in which you feel like the slightest trigger can send you over the edge and have you hurtling towards a suicidal vision.

The most effective metaphor I have to describe my feelings of that time is to ask you to picture me standing on a floor made entirely of glass. If something good happened to me, or if I had a good day with a friend or family member, the glass I was standing on would become a bit thicker, meaning that my resolve was stronger and I was less brittle. But if something bad happened, or if I had a setback or some kind of upsetting incident, cracks would start to appear in the glass. If those cracks ever became big or numerous enough, the glass floor would shatter and I would fall – in every sense of the word.

This metaphor is useful for a couple of reasons – firstly, the presence of a glass floor highlights the frailty of my level of wellbeing. Not only was it possible to look through the glass at what lay below, even the slightest structural deficiency could cause the glass to weaken and shatter. Have you ever heard of walking on eggshells around someone, so you don't hurt their feelings? It was like I was standing on eggshells myself, trying desperately not to upset my own sensibility. And secondly, it afforded me a symbolic base from which I could navigate my emotional and psychological limitations and capacities. Having this consistent self-awareness of how I was doing at any given moment was crucial in being able to take appropriate steps to help myself. But even with every safeguard in place, with every modicum of effort made to be aware of my psyche, it was still possible for everything to fall apart. In 2012, the glass floor beneath my feet shattered a few times. I firmly believe that if it weren't for the unyielding care of my family, friends and ex-girlfriend, I wouldn't have lasted long enough to write this book.

So why am I telling you this?

I believe that it important to share my experiences (on top of the anecdotes of interviewees) with you for a number of reasons.

Firstly, it is necessary to feature and provide insight into the struggles of those suffering from depression. By doing so, I hope that some, if not all of you, will be able to feel connected to what I know to be a relatively common story.

Secondly, I am trying to instil within law students and young legal professionals a sense of confidence and comfort in disclosing health issues. By discussing my own story so candidly and putting my name to it, I hope to inspire others. This does not mean that every young lawyer who has depression should go out and broadcast their experiences by writing a book; rather, the goal is to make those living with this condition feel safe enough to disclose their issues, and seek the help they need, without fear of personal or professional reprisal.

Finally, I am writing this so that we can all draw strength from the fact that things can get better. No matter how bad you feel, regardless of how awful things may appear, don't ever forget that it can get better. For me, it did. And with the right care, support and action, it will get better for you too. I truly hope that you can take something useful from this book, whether it is my story or my experiences, or the experiences of others.

At the very least, please give consideration to what is written here. After all, it could save your life, just as it did mine.

Legal Profession vs. Depression: Jerome's case for change

Lawyers are characterised as sitting "at the unenviable zenith of depressed professionals".[1]

Research and data indicates that "a happy life as a lawyer is much less about grades, affluence and prestige than about finding work that is interesting, engaging, personally meaningful, and focused on providing needed help to others".[2]

Consider both of these comments individually, and then in conjunction with one another. A cultural and environmental shift is clearly needed in order to better ensure the health and

1 Todd Peterson and Elizabeth Waters Peterson, "Stemming the Tide of Law Student Depression: What Law Schools Need to Learn from the Science of Positive Psychology" (2008), 9 (2) *Yale Journal of Health Policy, Law and Ethics* Article 2.

2 Lawrence S. Krieger and Kennon M. Sheldon, "What Makes Lawyers Happy?: A Data-Driven Prescription to Redefine Professional Success" (2015), 83 (2) *George Washington Law Review*, 592.

wellbeing of law students and young lawyers.

In 2013, John Brogden, former New South Wales Opposition Leader, addressed mental health issues in the legal field during the Tristan Jepson Memorial Foundation annual lecture. According to Brogden, lawyers are approximately three times more likely to report psychological distress than people in other industries.[3] This statistic is in direct correlation to the findings of the *Courting the Blues* report, which notes that at least 35 per cent of law students experience psychological distress while they are still in school[4] (as compared to one in six Australians nationwide).

Law school is, understandably, an arduous and taxing experience for those who undertake it. This is, by and large, a positive thing to the extent it aids one's personal and professional development. It should not, however, be so arduous and taxing as to spawn legal graduates who are suffering psychological distress.[5] Of course, the legal field is not the only industry that predisposes individuals to psychological distress.

Medicine, for example, also projects high levels of depression and anxiety. According to Dr Sally Cockburn, who is commonly known as "Dr Feel Good" in Australian medical media circles:

---

3 John Brogden, "Leading Change in the Legal Profession" (Speech delivered at the Tristan Jepson Memorial Foundation Annual Lecture 2013, Federal Court of Australia, 17 October 2013). <http://www.tjmf.org.au/2013/12/video-2013-tristan-jepson-memorial-foundation-annual-lecture/>

4 Dr Norman J. Kelk, Dr Georgina M. Luscombe, Dr Sharon Medlow and Professor Ian B. Hickie, *Courting the Blues: Attitudes towards depression in Australian law students and lawyers* (2009), BMRI Monograph 2009–1, Sydney: Brain & Mind Research Institute. <http://www.cald.asn.au/docs/Law%20Report%20Website%20version%204%20May%2009.pdf>

5 Molly Townes O'Brien, Stephen Tang and Kath Hall, "Changing our Thinking" (2011) 21 (1/2) *Legal Education Review*, 149.

"If you want to be a good doctor, you need to put effort into looking after yourself. You are not invincible – physically or mentally. The course can seem daunting and chip away at your self-worth, so you have to work at keeping your view of yourself in perspective. Because of the intense focus needed to get into medical school, many people stupidly sacrifice things that they enjoyed doing. Getting rid of hobbies is not a sign of self-discipline; it's actually counter-productive to your ultimate goal. In my experience, those people who keep up with their hobbies do better at medicine and life."[6]

The same is true for law students and young lawyers. There is little to no utility in sidetracking those parts of your life that bring purpose and joy to your existence. It is far more likely that you will be able to find motivation for studying and/or working if you are able to successfully balance your career pursuits, recreational activities and personal interests. This idea will be discussed at a greater length in later chapters.

Simply put, maintaining your hobbies will not only make your studying more productive, it will also make your law school experience more enjoyable. Isn't that worth striving for?

In discussing the importance of managing one's health and wellbeing in law, Dr Robert Fisher suggests individuals consider a three-tiered strategy.

"The more important thing, in my view, is understanding the principles of primary, secondary and tertiary prevention. The preventative measures that stop mental ill health developing in the beginning include reducing stress and bolstering your resilience so that you can cope with day-to-day vicissitudes of legal life.

"Getting appropriate expert help rapidly and complying with the treatment constitutes effective secondary prevention.

"Preventing relapse, which might mean leaving a toxic

6 Australian Medical Students' Association (AMSA) and New Zealand Medical Students' Association (NZMSA), "*Keeping your Grass Greener*" 4 <http://mentalhealth.amsa.org.au/wp-content/uploads/2014/08/KYGGWebVersion.pdf>

> *legal environment and going somewhere else, may be of marked assistance. Staying stable in mood, and not allowing unnecessary stress to cause you to decompensate you at work, is also critically important.*
>
> *"Taking regular breaks from work – daily, weekly and annually – is also critically important to maintaining good mental health and wellbeing, and that in turn may impact upon good physical health."*

I believe that most if not all law students and young lawyers are already up to date with primary prevention. It is the secondary preventative measures that this book intends to focus on, so that the tertiary undertakings are rendered unnecessary. This will not be realistic in all cases, of course; however it may be possible to change the course of events for some.

Signs and symptoms of depression in law

This book features the insights and anecdotes of dozens of legal professionals. What they have witnessed and experienced is paramount in the quest for you, the reader, to learn from your peers. To this end, I sourced a bevy of opinions on the relevant signs and symptoms of depression that you need to look out for.

Matthew Littlejohn (a junior lawyer at a mid-tier Australian commercial law firm):

> *"Common signs include withdrawal from social activities and making excuses to avoid seeing friends or other people, along with a change in sleeping or eating habits. A person suffering depression or anxiety will often try to distance themselves from others, usually so that others don't see that they're suffering. There may also be an increase in alcohol use, or using alcohol at inappropriate times e.g. getting drunk at lunch or before class.*
>
> *"The signs and symptoms can vary from person to person, though – some people, especially if they have suffered*

depression previously, can be good at masking their symptoms, and can sometimes go to the other extreme, being the soul of the party, so to speak, in an effort to convince others (and, often, themselves) that things are okay. The surest way to find out is to ask – and to not be afraid to ask if you think someone is suffering."

Aimee Riley (another junior lawyer at a different mid-tier Australian commercial law firm):

> *"I would say it is sometimes hard to pick the signs if you don't have some sort of relationship with the person. A change in behaviour is usually the most obvious sign – sudden lack of confidence, withdrawn from social events, always talking about work and what has to be done and how they are going to have to work late again – it is a combination of things really."*

Nick Edwards (a senior lawyer at a top-tier Australian commercial law firm and chair of an Australian-based charity):

> *"I think the first thing to acknowledge is that everyone will go through times of distress or anxiety – it is part and parcel of working in a fast moving, demanding environment. This in itself is not abnormal. It is when such periods become the norm that an issue in my mind arises. I also think there is no stereotypical suffering. Each person will have different indicators and from what I have seen or experienced people who are suffering from anxiety or distress tend to be prone to sleeplessness, stagnation of mood, lack of motivation, inability to focus and constant self-doubt. More importantly than the shopping list of 'signs' is being alert to change – that is, the student who was outgoing or talkative has over time regressed into their shell or the confident lawyer who was always first into the office who has now started to get in later and is sullen."*

Nathan Kennedy (a senior lawyer in a mid-tier Australian commercial law firm):

> *"The predominant sign I think is disengagement. It is noticeable when a person does not engage with colleagues and often will call in sick a lot. Conversely, I have also seen the opposite. It can manifest in a person trying to be too friendly with her colleagues. Of course there are more overt signs and I have had people openly upset about things at work. It is difficult to put into words but you often have a sense when someone is not happy."*

"Sunrise" (a fourth year law student who did not wish to be identified):

> *"I would say that sometimes depression and anxiety don't have identifiable symptoms. Your outward appearance in social settings is the same it always has been and you can muster a smile, a joke, maybe even laugh. Depression and anxiety are diseases that often strike strongest and hardest when you are on your own. Some identifiable symptoms include self-exclusion from social events, particularly last minute cancellations citing excuses such as 'I'm feeling ill' or 'something has come up, sorry!' If this is a recurrent occurrence, it may signal some battle with mental illness."*

Gavin Ingram (General Counsel for an international law practice):

> *"For me, I knew for a long time that things were not right. But I was too afraid to admit it to myself and too scared to let others know that I was not coping. What would they think? In fact, the hardest part was the need to be such a good actor to mask the symptoms. The constant fear, racing heart, nausea, dizziness and desire to just 'get out' had become my companion wherever I went and whatever I did. However, I had to continue going to work every day, to still work crazy hours and exude confidence and control on the outside. It was a different story on the inside. I knew when I felt too afraid to do things which other people wouldn't have given a second thought about that*

this could not go on. I was even nervous about walking down the street in case something happened.

"On my birthday in March 1998, a good friend phoned me and asked me if I wanted to go to lunch to celebrate. I lied and said I had a meeting. In truth, I just couldn't face the stress of being in public or in someone's presence if something 'did' happen to me. I hung up the phone and finally I broke down in tears. I finally picked up the telephone and called my mum. I had something I needed to tell her. My journey of healing had begun."

"J. McLeod" (a junior lawyer in a top-tier Australian commercial law firm):

"It varies from person to person and it's difficult to know without asking. But from personal experience, if you know someone who's been pulling a lot of late nights, has a big workload, lots of deadlines to meet and tends to take on too much, it's worth checking in with them every now and again to see how well they're balancing everything."

Senthorun Raj (a researcher at the University of Sydney Law School):

"Signs of depression and anxiety are not always visible. Many people who we see as 'happy' can be depressed. Personally, I think the best way to identify issues related to mental health is to be open, reflective, and non-judgemental when speaking to people."

Discussion of said signs and symptoms gives rise to consideration of the question, how are we to manage our health and wellbeing in law if the prevalent causes are unavoidable or inevitable? Thankfully, there are a number of strategies that one can implement which will be discussed in greater detail later in this book.

In the interim, however, one can mull over the words of Dr Fisher, who spoke of the need to have multiple strings to your bow in order to not only be a functioning legal professional, but a well-rounded person.

> *"If you're in a job about which you feel ambivalent, it is important to seek fulfilment, meaning and enjoyment from non-work related activities.*
>
> *"This is the responsibility you have to yourself. It is a wise thing to not have your eggs in one basket and to diversify your interests.*
>
> *"You should not just invest your whole self in the label, 'I am a lawyer.'*
>
> *"Hopefully you, as an individual, are a number of other things. You wear different hats, have different roles, and you get gratification from a number of different sources, not just from work."*

Adherence to such a mantra will, hopefully, place you in good stead to effectively manoeuvre your way through what can often seem like a minefield. In the case of *The Legal Profession vs. Depression*, you can be on the winning side!

> *"...Taking time to care for our mental health and wellbeing not only lessens our stress, it allows us to fully realise our potential to become better lawyers. The result is a legal practice that is not only sustainable and successful, but often a source of great satisfaction, joy and wisdom."*[7]

I feel that the above statement is incomplete – while it is important for law students and lawyers to maintain sufficient levels of emotional and mental health for professional purposes, it is more important to be healthy for the sake of your own happiness and wellbeing. As such, it is of fundamental importance that students be able to partake in holistic preventative healthcare measures as early as possible, so that

---

7 Joel Orenstein, "The mindful lawyer meditation and the practice of law" (2011) 85(7) *Law Institute Journal* 40.

they are better able to effectively maintain an appropriate work/life balance.

A high level of responsibility should lie with the individual to demand more from their law schools. The next generation of legal professionals must be embedded with a social justice consciousness, an existential philosophy to legal education and, most importantly, a holistic approach to one's health and wellbeing. Only through adherence to such ideas can today's law students evolve into well-rounded lawyers – the type of professionals our society needs and demands.

Why is there such a stigma about depression in law?

Since 1932, the United States military has awarded medals to soldiers who have been physically injured or killed by enemy combatants while serving in action. This medal is called the Purple Heart.

The advent of conflicts in the Middle East since the 1990s has seen a significant increase in the number of American military veterans diagnosed with, and treated for, post-traumatic stress disorder (PTSD). As a result of the increase in PTSD cases, numerous advocacy groups have argued that this and related illnesses should also be recognised when endowing a Purple Heart. In 2009, however, a US Department of Defense advisory committee determined that veterans suffering from psychological disorders such as PTSD would not be eligible for receipt of the medal, for the reason that such ailments are not intentionally caused by the enemy, nor are they objectively simple to diagnose, and/or recognise. Some veterans, who could receive a Purple Heart, would now be excluded as a result of the expanded criteria; shedding blood would be a prerequisite. This decision was supported by the Department of Defense itself, which surmised that virtue and honour should always be maintained.[8]

This draws similarities to the traditional mindset of the legal profession, which evokes the idea that mental health issues are demonstrative of a person's weakness, ignoring the fact that – at least in the example above – PTSD can last longer and be more devastating than cuts, bruises or a broken limb.

"Tess", a third year law student at the Australian National University, touched on this issue when she discussed the application process for special consideration for university exams and assessments:

> *"...There isn't always a lot of support in terms of things that you might get special consideration and extensions for. I think if you had a broken leg, it might be easier to get help from the law school. I've applied for special consideration and not received it, and it's fine, it has always worked out okay in the end, but you sort of see it as a bigger gap between professors and students, than it would be in other areas."*

This discussion demonstrates that societal impressions on issues like psychological distress, anxiety and depression are not fully understood or appreciated by those who do not suffer from them, because no physical symptoms can be clearly identified (unless the person exhibits evidence of self-harm). And, as such, in the mind of a layman, these issues may or do not exist.

Unfortunately, this attitude can also be applicable to other sectors of society. Issues like psychological distress, anxiety

---

8 Michael Sandel, Justice: *What's the right thing to do?* (Penguin Books Ltd, 2009) 10–11.

and depression are frequently referenced, particularly in the media, as being private, confidential matters that relate to relevant individuals[9] and thus must be dealt with as such. It is no surprise, therefore, that many law students and young lawyers fear the potential consequences of speaking up about the health issues (psychological, emotional and/or physical) they may be experiencing. In fact, these individuals tend to view these types of ailments as stigmatising and prejudicial, in regards to employment and success,[10] and as a result they are left to their own devices when "solving" the problems at hand.

I now understand that, but for my disclosure about my health problems, I would not have been able to experience the enriching and stimulating jobs I have had over the past few years, nor would I have grown into the type of person I am today. As a result, I am tremendously driven towards showing law students and young lawyers that they should muster the courage to come forward, if they feel the need.

This chapter explores the stigma attached to mental health issues. I acknowledge and applaud the progress that has been made by the legal profession in raising awareness and providing support to embattled lawyers, but until every young member of the law profession feels confident enough to speak up, this will continue to be a pressing issue.

Should I be fearful of my chosen profession?

Danny Gilbert, managing partner of a top-tier Australian commercial law firm, has a wide-reaching perception of how attitudes towards depression have evolved over time. It is

9 Kelk et al, n 4.

10 Penny Watson and Rachael Field, "Promoting Student Wellbeing and Resilience at Law School" in Sally Kift, Jill Cowley, Michelle Sanson and Penny Watson (eds), *Excellence and Innovation in Legal Education* (Federation Press, 2011) 395.

encouraging to read his words because they imply that we, as a profession, are headed in the right direction.

> *"I think there is a much greater acceptance of it than there was; I'm not saying there's not further to go. There is certainly much more acceptance than when I was a young lawyer. Indeed, there is greater acceptance in the community more generally. When I was growing up as a kid in the country, I never heard of the word 'depression'."*

But there is no doubting there is still a long way to go.

Graeme Cowan is an internationally renowned author and speaker with expertise in building resilience, creating robust and thriving cultures, and aiding workplace stress management. Prior to his newfound success, however, a psychiatrist described Graeme's experience with depression as the worst case he had ever seen.

In research for *The Elephant in the Boardroom*, Graeme's most recent project about stigma about mental health issues, he made some unsettling findings:

> *"Eighty-six per cent of people with a mood disorder would rather suffer in silence than discuss their condition with work colleagues. Many fear that disclosing a mental illness will lead to workplace exclusion and compromised career prospects, and with 83 per cent of respondents reporting experiencing stigma in some form as a result of their mood disorder, this fear is not without merit."*[11]

James Tobin, a partner at a mid-tier Australian commercial law firm, notes that it can be difficult to shake off long-standing impressions that have ultimately formed the cultural and/or environmental atmosphere of law school or a law firm.

> *"In the last five years, we have moved a long way in the legal profession towards confronting these issues, but I still think*

11 Graeme Cowan, *The Elephant in the Boardroom: Getting Mentally Fit for Work* (Executive Summary) (2013), 2.

> *there is a stigma, which is attached to it wrongly with a number of members of the profession who are of the older years, who* [are under the impression] *that it will never happen to them – mental health issues happen to other people and it's not a health issue. There is still a lot of misunderstanding, and a lot of uneducated people out there, who don't understand that it can happen to anyone, and there's no reason or rhyme as to how it happens, and why it happens, and that it can really affect anyone. Unfortunately I think they probably still believe the stigma associated with it, but I can say that the law field has done a lot of education over the years, and is moving in the right direction, and I think society is far more educated now. They understand that one in three lawyers is going to suffer from some form of mental illness at some stage in their lives."*

Professor Maxine Evers, Associate Dean (Education) for the Faculty of Law at the University of Technology, Sydney, sees it in a slightly different way. According to Maxine, people's attitudes may be shifting with regards to depression, and there may be greater acceptance of ill health, but in a lot of professional environments where commercial and fiscal viabilities drive business, any potential mark against an individual can be costly. This does not make it right, or even justified.

> *"I still think that there still is a stigma about people, and you could draw an analogy with women of a certain age, childbearing ages, that are in workplaces. There's a question about, 'If we take this person on, they're going to fall pregnant, they're going to want to have maternity leave, or if it's a male, if they're starting a family, they're going to want paternity leave.' You know, someone who might have some health issues, there's still a concern about, if you're looking at it from a commercial perspective, that there's some issues around productivity."*

So even if the personal and emotional stigma is decreasing, albeit slowly, there may still remain a professional and commercial concern. It is perfectly reasonable, as such, for an individual to be worried about how their employer perceives them, following a disclosure of ill health.

Given these facts, how can you feel comfortable about sharing any health issues that you are experiencing with your employer? "Louise", a lawyer with a mid-tier Australian commercial law firm who requested that her name be withheld, believes it is important to share, especially if your goal is to help the community understand and appreciate any issues. Not only should there not be a stigma about mental health issues but there should also be an acknowledgement that actually talking about them will reap positive benefits.

> *"I think that depression, or mental health issues are everywhere. It's a really high rate, and I think it should be talked about more. Two people very close to me have depression, and I really enjoy talking to them about it, so I can learn about what it's like, and how it must be for them to deal with it. I don't understand why it's not talked about more. I've always been supportive of people who know that I want to talk about it."*

Troy Douglas, law graduate turned entrepreneur, discussed the idea of being confident in yourself, and not allowing anyone else's impressions or feelings to dictate how you perform your day-to-day functions. And he's right – by owning your personal situation, and developing an awareness of how to best look after yourself, you will convey a sense of independence, and a self-sustainability that will not only endear you to others, but will be enviable.

> *"I think owning your situation and your emotional state is the best way to overcome a negative stigma placed on you by others. In other words, I think everybody is concerned about his or her professional integrity, and how they're viewed. That is a natural thing. But think of the Taylor Swift lyrics, 'Haters gonna*

hate'. From personal experience, I was starting a business, and studying law, and then I came out as being gay, and I dealt with it more easily than people, who struggled with that stuff for a long time. And, for me, it was because I already owned the situation.

"I think if you are speaking openly about it, you own it by saying, 'I'm a bit overwhelmed right now. I've got too much stuff going on,' in a professional workplace environment the people above you, in the hierarchy of the office, will make it work to your benefit. If you hide it, it'll be a negative because it will be seen as you're not able to understand yourself."

Sarah Beth, a legal services professional with experience in a range of different fields, advocates a strategic approach. She asserts that while negative attitudes may be dissipating, it is still important to pick your audience when confiding in someone. In other words, as long as you have a solid, supportive network around you, you will be able to navigate the professional landscape.

"It's affirming to see perceptions or stigmas surrounding depression and anxiety are actually changing, for the better – particularly in the workplace. Many workplaces now offer accessible and confidential programs including counselling frameworks embedded with support initiatives and/or strategies to assist you on this journey. Investing time in yourself to create a tailored plan, whether you choose to access workplace programs or find help outside your place of employment (which may be enhanced by the support of a qualified professional), and discerning which elements resonate best with you, will be of great assistance when you aren't sure where to start.

"Whether you choose to disclose your situation professionally, to an employer, colleague or a mentor, or personally, within your circle of family and/or friends, it's important to have a trusted network of people you can share your experience with, a safe place where to bounce ideas off, gain insight and assurance, debrief and gain perspective. With time, patience and intuition, making small steps toward the practice of self-care, self-

advocacy and building a strong support network will provide immense value."

Nick Ferrari, a junior lawyer in a top-tier Australian commercial law firm, expounds on this idea, when explaining how transparency and honesty in his life resulted in an acceptance that health issues may simply be a part of a person's life, and there is no stigma to be attached. What this means, ultimately, is that it is crucial for you to be surrounded by people who exhibit empathy and compassion towards you, and with whom you have a good rapport should these types of issues arise.

> *"I've had a lot of experience with mental health issues from when I was quite young. Some of my close family and friends have experienced quite severe mental health issues. I've seen it first hand, and for me it's not something I see as being stigmatised. In some senses I'm lucky as well because the firm that I'm at have taken a number of very proactive steps to recognise that mental health is an issue and take steps to make it acceptable for people to talk about it, manage their mental health, and deal with it when it does come up."*

TWD Wellbeing Wisdom

Dr Fisher offers a sound summation of the stigmatised perception of mental illness – not just within the legal profession, but also throughout society as a whole.

> *"There is the stigma that comes from being different, being odd, being dangerous, but there is another side to this situation. You may be seen as weak or vulnerable, not be 'one of us'. Your colleagues or managers may believe you cannot be relied upon, that you're going to get sick and not come back to work. They may also think that you could cause trouble in the work place.*
>
> *"Now, some of these comments can be true – there are some people with mental illness who will not be able to return fully mentally fit. Nonetheless, the vast majority of individuals who have these conditions are amenable to treatment and they can also be capable of performing at their previous high levels of functioning, and indeed in some cases, through psychotherapy plus medication, they can achieve not only stability but they may be capable of performing at a far higher level than before they became sick."*

Given this widespread perception, it can be hard to know exactly how to respond if you find yourself encumbered by ill health. Graeme Cowan offers a strategic approach to manage this.

> *"Only tell someone you trust because there's still are big issues around disclosing at the workplace. So if they have an environment that does welcome that disclosure and people being authentic, I think you should feel comfortable to share it, but I really advise people to only with people you trust."*

Stigma about these health issues may still exist, depending on the workplace. However, this does not mean that you should feel scared of coming forward if you develop depression or related ailments; rather, know how and when to disclose your health condition, so that you remain in the best position (personally and professionally).

I don't have depression. Why should I worry?

Australians are more susceptible to skin cancer than persons in other nations because of the country's geographical climate and exposure to ultra-violet rays. As such, we Australians are advised to apply sunscreen before heading to the beach, or even going outside on a summer's day. Similarly, I believe that those in the legal profession need to apply the same logic to managing our emotional and psychological wellbeing given the high rates of depression that exist in our chosen field.

As was touched on earlier in the book, more than one-third (over 35 per cent) of law students report experiencing disturbingly high levels of psychological distress, anxiety and depression while in law school. The enormity of this statistic is highlighted by the fact that approximately 18 per cent of students studying medicine, a field that is similar to law in regards to prevalent health issues, report experiencing similar problems. Overall, approximately 13 per cent of university students, from the general population, report experiencing some level of psychological distress, anxiety and/or depression while enrolled in tertiary study.[12]

This book addresses a range of significant issues that law students and young lawyers face, while in school, and once they enter the legal field. Some of these issues can be quite overwhelming and stressful. It is imperative that each individual recognises that their study and practice of work, by virtue of environment, increases their vulnerability to psychological issues, like anxiety and depression. Some may not recognise that they are at risk and may have their health problems go undetected.

A professional sportsman understands that he or she has a greater chance of sustaining physical injuries; therefore, he or she stretches intensely before exerting him or herself on the field. The rest of us, who may simply play sports socially, often turn up for the games five minutes before the start – running onto the field without loosening up our muscles. And for the most part that's okay! But when you are properly entrenched in that environment as we, law students and lawyers, are, it is necessary to take certain measures to ensure we can be at our best.

There are lawyers who skate through their legal careers without ever facing hardships and issues. These lucky individuals appear to experience success even when they fail to complete hypothetical pre-game stretching routines. However, there are others, who neglect to take proactive steps to take care of themselves until it is too late. As a result, these individuals have a higher risk of developing physical and/or mental health conditions. I am targeting these individuals

12 Kelk et al, n 4.

with this chapter.

The importance of being proactive

Be aware, be mindful and most of all be active.

Whether it is alluded to as a cultural impression in this book or spoken about in the workplace or on-campus, all legal professionals are aware of the idea that one's employer may view having an illness such as depression as a "weakness" or "failure". Leaving aside the ridiculousness of such an idea for one minute, I note that, in a further twist of irony, I can identify that perhaps the failure that I experienced was not that I had become ill – it was that I was unable to recognise it and deal with it. I say all of this not to scare you, but to equip you with the perspective necessary to go out and take charge of your own situation; by taking a proactive approach to your health and wellbeing in law, you give yourself the best possible chance of staying healthy and happy.

Professor Paul Redmond (former Dean of the University of New South Wales Law School):

> *"Prevention is a bit better than a cure, and I think it's very sensible for people to anticipate that the nature of their study or their work might dispose them towards negative feelings and negative sentiments, and even doubting ones, pressing ones, and so going on the front foot and being active, being engaged, having friends, having interests, and prioritising always will, I think, be sensible for everyone."*

"Louise":

"…It doesn't hurt to proactively manage your health, in any facet of your life, whatever stage you're in."

Luke Furness (a junior lawyer in a top-tier Australian commercial law firm):

"Just as you take out health insurance in case of skiing accidents, so could your situation deteriorate, and you could show signs of clinical depression, and as such, you need to be aware of that condition. And, perhaps, it is being aware of the difference between having a bad day and having a row of bad days, and having a bad client and showing symptoms that suggests that you might have mental distress in a way that's diagnosable. And I guess the other way that it could become relevant is by helping others see the signs, and treading lightly over people, who are experiencing the signs of mental distress."

Lauren Fitzpatrick (a junior governmental lawyer):

"I think being proactive is the best way to go about anything. Just because somebody thinks that they might be immune to becoming mentally ill, even if they think they are immune to becoming physically ill, you never know when something might hit you. You don't want to risk something like that happening, because it could have a detrimental impact on yourself, and your family and friends.

"Taking proactive measures will benefit you in the long run, such as playing sport, and having a strong and supportive network of family and friends. I believe these will impact you positively as a person as well."

Brendan O'Brien (Special Counsel for an international law firm):

"I can totally understand why someone would say, 'I don't need help' and feel that they are bulletproof, and it's fair to take that view before you start your career or at the beginning of your career. However, the reality is that at some point in your career, if not at several points, you're going find the going

> *pretty hard from a mental health point of view. It's probably not a very nice thing for a young law student to hear, but if you accept that the incidence of depression in law is greater than in other professions, then you've got to accept that there's a good chance that it is going to happen to you. It's not necessarily something to worry about, but to at least to be aware of and to know how you can get assistance if necessary."*

"Katherine" (a senior lawyer in the Australian Public Service who requested anonymity):

> *"When you are reacting, you are having issues, so wouldn't it be good to have tools [to proactively manage your health] before you have the issues? I have to say that I now draw on those tools all the time and they prevent me from having incidents again. I mean, you have bouts of depression in your life, it just happens, but having the tools to work through it is crucial."*

All six of the interviewees are right. You have nothing to lose by proactively being self-aware (looking out for yourself). In fact, you have everything to gain!

This discussion is not intended to intimidate lawyers and law students, or scare them into taking action. That would be, without a doubt, counter-productive to this entire exercise. Instead, let's just take this conversation for what it is – a recognition of the statistics regarding prevalence, and an acknowledgement that individuals can and should take a greater responsibility for themselves. Marie Jepson encapsulates the importance of self-care and care for others, and drives this point home.

> *"You may think that this won't happen to you – that you are immune, but stress has a cumulative effect, its symptoms often developing over time. In* Courting the Blues *both lawyers and law students identify avoidable workplace stress as a major*

contributor to their depression and mental ill health. Creating a psychologically healthy and safe workplace benefits everyone – not just those who are unwell. It's really quite simple. Healthy people work better, are more productive and efficient as well as caring about their colleagues and demonstrating pro-social behaviour."

Joel Orenstein writes:

"...Our problem, as lawyers, is that we so often neglect to attend to our own thoughts and emotions. In the process, we are missing opportunities for more effective lawyering, and at the same time our mental health is suffering..."[13]

Many law firms, both large and small, have put initiatives into action that combat depression within the workplace. In addition, law faculties within a number of Australian universities now offer on-campus programs that directly or indirectly purport to facilitate the wellbeing of students as they journey through tertiary education.

These initiatives are crucial and necessary for the wellbeing of legal practitioners. It is extremely important that these individuals be introduced to the initiatives while they are still in the initial stages of their legal careers. During this time, they are better able to develop good habits that will persist throughout their lifetimes. Preventative measures are more effective in countering issues like depression, than trying to resolve them after they have arisen. It is a two-way street, however. Your educational institution or employer can implement as many programs and safeguards as it wants, but if you, as an individual, are unwilling to engage with the material, you will not get much benefit out of them.

13 Orenstein, n 7.

Here is where we return to the idea of taking responsibility for one's self. A junior lawyer for a top-tier Australian commercial law firm, who wished to be referred to as "Robert James", discussed this issue.

> *"Personal responsibility, I think, is the cornerstone of being successful in law. But at the same time one needs to look after one's neighbour. So both really go hand-in-hand. As much as a person should be pro-active in looking after his or her own physical wellbeing, so should the environment, in which he or she studies or works. So it's really a combination of individual and social responsibility."*

To be clear, I am not suggesting that if individuals do not look out for themselves and each other, they will have no one to blame. That assumption is not the end goal of this point. What I am trying to reinforce is that individuals, including myself, should be empowered to take charge of their own existence, and not allow life to dictate who they are and/or who they will become. Issues such as psychological distress, anxiety and depression are dissimilar from physical injuries such as cuts and bruises in a number of ways. But in light of this discussion, the most important disparity is the fact that those physical injuries are easily identifiable and recognisable. Because psychological ailments do not come to the surface in the same way, they can go undetected until it is perhaps too late. Kate Taylor, a law graduate turned financial professional, gives an interesting take on how legal professionals should therefore approach this situation, regardless of how they may be feeling on any given day.

> *"I don't see mental illness as being black and white; that you either have one or you don't. I think throughout our lives you will sit on a scale, a continuum, if you will; and you can fluctuate on that continuum depending on what happens or how you're feeling. And I think, at any time you can be feeling great, then two weeks down the track not be feeling so good. As such,*

anyone can be affected by mental illness at any time."

Give yourself the best possible chance to be master of your own (legal) destiny.

> *"It is...unrealistic to entirely reduce the causes of stress in law school or in legal practice, so it is important to provide law students with knowledge and skills on how to cope with the usual causes of chronic stress and maladaptive stress patterns."*[14]

While we may never be able to completely remove the problem, it is of fundamental importance to at least equip students and graduates with the tools and knowledge necessary to prevent and/or combat any issues of health and wellbeing, should they arise. Furthermore, by arming students and graduates with the necessary tools, they will be better equipped for the workplace, more well-rounded and holistically focused legal professionals, thereby making them subsequently more employable.

---

14 Colin James and Jenny Finlay-Jones, "I Will Survive: Strategies for Improving Lawyers' Workplace Satisfaction" (2007), 15(1) *Legal Education Digest* 32 <http://papers.ssrn.com/sol3/papers.cfm?abstract_id=2320353>

TWD Wellbeing Wisdom

Dr Fisher concurs with the notion of proactivity rather than reactivity. In discussion of how best to promote this idea from a medical standpoint, he suggests that law students and young lawyers be aware of the following.

> *"People need to understand that probably the majority of episodes of psychiatric illness are triggered by perceived stress, and the individual's threshold for becoming stressed varies across a continuum. Vulnerability to high levels of adrenaline and cortisol varies across a continuum.*
>
> *"Primary prevention means effectively eliminating stressful factors or building your resilience in the face of what you perceive to be stressful. So often it is a matter of utilising cognitive and behavioural techniques to alter the way you view the world and view yourself.*
>
> *"Often there can be a sustained period of stress, or the sudden confrontation with a particular event, or series of events, in a concentrated period of time, which triggers psychological and emotional decompensation.*
>
> *"Being self-reflective about these patterns is a critical part of ongoing self-care."*

In addition to speaking with individual legal professionals, I also sought input from a national advocacy body – the Australian Law Students' Association (hereafter "ALSA").

> *"ALSA encourages law students and young lawyers to take proactive measures to ensure that they are managing their health and wellbeing because, as the saying goes, 'prevention is better than cure'. While educational institutions and workplaces bear some onus in promoting a healthy study and work environment for students and young lawyers, we also urge students to take personal ownership over their wellbeing and to implement measures and strategies which ensure that one's*

mental health is held to be a priority – to the same degree, if not greater – than studies and work commitments."

Research conducted in the United States showed that, not unlike the situation in Australia, lawyers are 3.6 times more likely to suffer from psychological distress, anxiety, and depression than the rest of the employed population. And, as a result, lawyers also have a greater risk of suffering from heart disease, alcoholism, and substance abuse/drug addiction.[15] Although these issues may never affect you, it doesn't mean that you shouldn't be aware of the personal, cultural, environmental or professional factors that may increase your likelihood of developing such issues.

For the same reason that Australians need to wear sunscreen to avoid skin cancer when they go to the beach, young legal professionals need to take steps to manage their health and wellbeing, so as to avoid depression and other psychological issues.

No young lawyer or law student should fear mental health issues. Such fear only exacerbates your current state of anxiety. But you do need to be aware, and subsequently arm yourself, with the practical tools needed to be healthy and happy.

15 Peterson et al, n 1, 358.

If law can be bad for your health, why do it?

Abraham Lincoln, the 16th president of the United States, is well remembered for his role in both presiding over the American Civil War and the abolition of slavery, as well as being one of four American presidents to have been assassinated. A lesser-known fact about President Lincoln, however, is that he suffered from depression. Lincoln was, by all reports as far as others could tell, not depressed in his early life. He was, by nature, a worrier, which emerged more visibly upon his encounter with a certain professional strand:

> *"These streaks of sadness and worry may have been minor depressions. But it wasn't until 1835 that serious concerns emerged about Lincoln's health...the first sign of trouble came*

with his intense study of the law."[16]

If Abraham Lincoln was able to achieve everything that he did in his lifetime, despite his depression, there is no reason why you too cannot also manage any form of this condition, and still be the legal professional that you want to be.

Let's be very clear about this – you have the ability to do whatever you want to do with your life. Fear of what may be cannot dictate how you choose to live your personal and/or professional life, regardless of what direction you wish to take. "Palm Tree", a junior governmental lawyer, aptly summarises this:

> *"I wouldn't avoid law just because…I wouldn't let fear of ill health stop me from enrolling in a law degree program. I mean, it is a great degree to have, and law is a great profession to work in."*

Law is, without question, one of the broadest and most diverse careers that one can explore. But in light of everything being discussed in this book, why should you continue to pursue this career path? Look at this way – if the reports are correct, which state that the rates of anxiety and depression skyrocket within the year of law school, then, you could be forgiven for wanting to give up, and simply go elsewhere. That is definitely one option, but it may not be the *best* option for you if law is what you truly want to be doing. Why not? Well, because there are many benefits associated with the study and/or practice of law. In fact, the interviewees referenced in this chapter became passionate and excited when talking about how law is a worthwhile profession.

16 Joshua Wolf Shenk, *Lincoln's Melancholy: How depression challenged a president and fuelled his greatness* (Houghton Mifflin Co, 2005) 18.

What can the study and practice of law give you?

"Robert James" offered a rational response to why a person should weigh their options, before deciding whether or not to enter the law field.

> *"Life involves risks, and can be quite harsh in its consequences. Law, in particular, has serious risks associated with it (risks that are greater than in any other profession). However, the study of law teaches you about society, and the way it is ordered. Moreover, one can carve out a career in law that encompasses a variety of different subfields. You can also be immensely satisfied with your career choice, because it allows you to understand people, in general, much better. And when you understand people, you can make a real difference in the world."*

Ultimately, it is going to come down to you, and what you want from your life. "Robert James" is right – life does involve risks – and sometimes they are unavoidable. But unless that risk is immediately threatening to yourself or others, there shouldn't be much standing in your way of trying to achieve your goals. Personally, I see great benefit in having studied a law degree, and thus having sought and received the qualification to practise law in my home state of New South Wales. Such educational and professional standing affords me options that I otherwise would not have. Regardless of the health issues I have encountered, I do not regret the choices I made for one second. You can also look at it from a more individual perspective, rather than through the lenses of another person. Why should external circumstances or environmental factors dictate the path you choose? Especially if you have your heart set on a particular career?

Professor Jill McKeough, former Dean of Law at the University of Technology, Sydney, and Commissioner for the Australian Law Reform Commission, discusses the importance of law in society and how this can overwhelm any feeling of trepidation:

> *"I've never felt that I needed to question the value of my job. Law is an essential underpinning, especially if people can understand what it means to have the rule of law operating in their society. It's about the way the world works, it interferes with everything we do, it's what regulates us, it's what creates our society and nothing works without it."*

Taking such an approach in perceiving the value of your work can be critical. "Eleanor Robinson", a public sector criminal law solicitor who requested anonymity, is of a similar mindset in espousing that the professional skills that she acquired continuously fuel her interest in law.

> *"I love what I do because I love being analytical. I like reading the way our law has progressed, and I like looking at arguments and legislation, and piecing it all together with facts. I have a career that really excites me, because I want to help people. I certainly don't think that because you get a law degree, you have to become a lawyer, and that is the good thing about studying it – it opens up doors – there is no denying it. If you end up loving it, and you gain experience and it makes you happy – go for it! It will reward you, and you will be challenged, and it is so interesting. It is a great industry to be a part of."*

Lucinda Clarke, associate for an international commercial law firm, supported the comments of "Eleanor Robinson" by discussing how studying law can be and is a valuable asset in your professional development.

> *"I will never regret doing my law degree. My mother always said once you have a law degree, no one can take it away from you, and that, in itself, is a very powerful feeling. It can open doors to a lot of different jobs. Nor will I regret my years at my previous law firm. It was a fantastic place for training and groundwork, and experience that I am not sure I would have, otherwise,*

received from another job."

It is important to maintain an appreciation for law, especially if you want to avoid ill health. In fact, the study and practice of law are choices you probably will never regret. The educational and vocation benefits associated with the law field are exceptional and amazing, for the right person. This career choice will never be considered a waste of time (at least for most). In addition, you can take solace in the fact that even, if you occasionally come across difficult times, you will be intellectually and professionally prepared as a result of your law experiences.

"Sunrise" offers an intriguing perspective on this topic. Despite the somewhat crude depiction of what might be, she maintains a positive perspective, when it comes to studying, volunteering, and working.

> *"As much as I hate the law sometimes, I ultimately love it. I love the friends, and I love the extracurricular activities. I can get involved in volunteering overseas, and/or I can get involved helping people. It's very rewarding. I think it's one of the most rewarding and satisfying careers you can have.*
>
> *"It's also very empowering. I feel empowered that I will never put myself in a position, whereby, something bad can happen, because I know about the law. And it is empowering, in the sense of something small. For instance, stores sometimes say to customers, 'You can't exchange that, or can't get refund, without a receipt.' And I can say, 'Well, actually I can. I want a refund for this shirt, so give me my money back!' It's a very good way to protect yourself, so even if you don't work in a legal field, knowledge of the law can be very beneficial."*

Nick Edwards works longer hours than most lawyers, yet he still maintains a passion for his work that is rather enviable. According to Nick, working such long hours can sometimes cease to matter; if you find yourself consumed by the daily issues your encounter.

> *"It is a wonderful career because it is engaging, it's interesting, and it's challenging. It makes you think creatively, and it provides you with a great deal of satisfaction, as a career choice. You work with the 'best of the best' a lot of the times, and you work with people who look at the world the same way you do – in a very logical, practical way."*

Nathan Kennedy elaborates on Nick's assertion:

> *"I like being a lawyer. I don't always like everything that I do in the office, because it can be a bit boring, but it's not that I dislike being a lawyer. I've always liked practising law, and sometimes, you know you'll always go through periods in which you say, 'This is boring – I've been in the office three weeks running, and I haven't even gotten out.' But the thought of not practising law actually makes me sad. So if you like to practise law, then it's very rewarding, even though you have your 'down days' like everyone else. But if you don't like it, then I'd say you probably still have a lot of options."*

While the workload can be imposing for a legal professional, it can also provide a worthy challenge, both intellectually and physically, for a law student or young lawyer. In fact, Ashleigh Fehrenbach, a junior lawyer in a mid-tier Australian commercial law firm, talked about how these demands can exhilarate and help you evolve into a better lawyer.

> *"Working in law can be difficult and challenging, but it's also mentally very stimulating and rewarding. You get to be surrounded be some incredible people throughout law school as well as when you're working. I don't mean that just in terms of intelligence. You will be surrounded by people who have similar interests to you and that's very motivating. It's very challenging but rewarding as well."*

I too have found in situations in which I am working on something that enthralls and captivates me to the point where the volume of work or the hours expended cease to matter. If you are able to find a niche in law whereby you can extrapolate such satisfaction from your work, then you have – to use a colloquial term – "made it".

It is not wise to be so intensely focused on your work all of the time. But as in any professional environment, the occasional challenge can be stimulating and character building. In fact, there is no shortage of opportunities in the law field, which is very enticing!

There is also a range of community-based reasons to pursue a career in law.

Luke Furness touched on the more altruistic aspects of law, and how the study and practice of law can give rise to a professional environment, in which you can make a tangible difference in society.

> *"I think a more substantial reason to pursue law is social justice; it's a very good reason to get into law, if you have a charitable mind. I think another reason is policy development, especially if you want to change the law, and make law better. And, then, I think a good understanding of the technical rules of law is essential to your journey. I think another one is just the pure, intellectual stimulation of law – liking the law for the sake that it's the law. We have some good conversations that are relevant to your degree, like jurisprudence and legal theory type arguments. It is actually really enjoyable, at the end of the day, to study law. And then I guess the generality of law isn't really a bad reason to study law either. If you're not sure, or you think you are more about developing skills, then law may be a good general degree to ultimately base your career on."*

This is where I have discovered the greatest joy from my experiences in law. If you are able to utilise your skills and knowledge in a manner that serves the greater good, that enhances society's commitment to justice and order, that upholds the rule of law, then you are doing something worthwhile with your legal career.

There is also another way that we can examine this entire issue. What if law could actually have a positive impact on your health and wellbeing?

Senthorun Raj discusses how studying law, and working as a legal academic, has given him emotional and intellectual benefits that he, otherwise, may not have been able to receive.

> *"I would argue that in many ways, the skills I've developed have developed my confidence, my capacity to engage with other people, which has empowered my standing and my personal health. And so, in some ways, I don't necessarily agree with that kind of statement. What I will say, though, is that people just need to be able to find what matters to them and ask themselves whether what they're doing is meaningful to them and to other people. And if their answer to that question is a 'no', regardless of what it is, it's probably time to reassess."*

Terry McCabe, the principal for a mid-tier Australian commercial law firm, espoused his love for the law, and why he finds his work to be so rewarding. Reading over his response, you can tell how enriching and influential law has been in his life, without which he may not have had such a gratifying career.

> *"I have never had a day when I have gotten up in the morning, and thought, 'I don't want to go into work today'. I really love what I am doing, even with all of the baggage. So to me, it is absolutely worth it. There is nothing more enjoyable or intellectually satisfying than facing a challenge, and being able to work together to achieve a solution that provides a better outcome.*

> *"That's what law aims to do, whether it's a criminal that has been charged with breaking and entering, or an old couple wanting to manage their estate planning in a way that protects their assets for a disabled child. Or, whether you are a company director trying to achieve the best outcome from a merger, or you are a legislator seeking to effect a parliamentary will, I love our profession. I'm so pleased that that person from the universities admission centre steered me this way, because it was absolutely the correct way to go."*

So this leaves us with the thoughts of Lauren Fitzpatrick, who wraps up the chapter in a manner that is both heartwarming and motivating.

> *"Law is such an amazing degree. It's so interesting, and it's really challenging, but it's a good challenge. As long as you have everything balanced, the chance that you could suffer from a mental illness shouldn't put you off from enrolling in the course. There is a lot of support out there for students and lawyers. Law's a great degree, and everyone that I know who has studied law and moved into the profession absolutely loves it."*

As mentioned previously, I do not recommend that you allow fear to dictate how you shape your professional development. If you want to do something, you should do your best to make it happen. Take preventative measures for your health and wellbeing along the way, and you will be just fine!

TWD Wellbeing Wisdom

The prevalence of psychological distress, anxiety, and depression in law is undoubtedly disquieting for any prospective law student or young lawyer, so much so that one may be put off the study and practice of law altogether. But judging by the constructive answers given by our interviewees, it is clear that there are plenty of practical positives to be gleaned from a career in law.

If ever you find yourself intimidated by the prospect of a legal career, research what this vocation can do for you. Until then consider the following:

- Law is a fruitful, vocational avenue because it opens up so many doors for you professionally.
- The personal and professional skills you develop can give rise to invigorating and inspiring work.
- If you have a genuine interest in law, health and wellbeing issues can be assuaged by your underlying passions and gifts.
- You can make a meaningful impact on the communities around you (through use of your legal skills and knowledge).
- If you are able to find your niche, your chosen vocation may significantly improve your wellbeing and happiness.
- And as long as you have given proper consideration to the "pros and cons" of a particular professional avenue, there is no reason why you cannot succeed in your work, both personally and professionally!

The direction that your legal career takes should be reflective of your own passions, gifts and values. If you choose a path that best suits you and your needs, there is no reason why the profession should be anything other than fulfilling for your personal and professional psyche. Dr Fisher offers succinct advice on this front.

"Know yourself, know what you're getting into, and run your own race."

Personalities, Part I: Identifying our legal idiosyncrasies

Whenever I discuss the motivation behind the writing of this book with others, I explain the prevalence and effects of depression in law, and what I perceive to be the subsequent need for this book in the market. In response, the first thing people always ask is: Why do so many legal professionals suffer from depression? As this book details, there are many reasons why this is the case. One thing I have found is that certain personality traits are among the most fascinating factors in justifying why depression in law is such an issue.

In 2009, the *Legal Education Review* identified traits that make law students and lawyers more vulnerable to mental illness, as opposed to their counterparts in other job industries:

- They are more likely to see employers as interested in their marks, and not in other social characteristics such as: personal code of ethics, ability to communicate, and/or leadership skills;

- They are more likely to see their friendships in terms of networks (as a way to advance their careers);
- They tend to dislike group work (as learning and grading methods);
- They tend to view their grades as the most important motivators and indicators of success;
- They are less likely to find their studies intrinsically interesting; and
- They are more likely to be highly "perfectionistic" (Note: There is strong evidence that perfectionism can lead to relationship difficulties).[17]

The three most common idiosyncrasies that our interviewees pinpointed as being associated with the psyche of law students and young lawyers were:

- Pessimism;
- Perfectionism;
- Competitiveness.

This chapter will explore the ways, in which our interviewees perceived these traits, what effects these traits can have on an individual, and how those of us in the legal profession should regard these issues.

Pessimism

It is widely accepted across almost all professional occupations that people who are optimistic perform better than those who are pessimistic. There is one exception to this rule – the legal profession, where it has been proven that people with pessimistic tendencies significantly outperform optimists.[18]

17 Massimiliano Tani and Prue Vines, "Law Students' Attitudes to Education: Pointers to Depression in the Legal Academy and Profession?" (2009) *Legal Education Review* 3.

18 Peterson et al, n 1, 358.

Skills such as analytical thinking, having the ability to look for flaws in arguments or evidence, and being critical and meticulous of the facts are basic tenets for all lawyers; however, optimism is generally an accurate indicator of a person's happiness, resilience, and motivation.[19]

What, then, are we to make of pessimistic traits in law?

Paul Redmond:

> *"Much of legal work is around anticipating and avoiding unwelcome outcomes and in transactional work guarding against them by appropriate documentation; even in a litigation practice, a sense of pessimism, a sense of what might be an undesirable outcome, is a strategic advantage."*

"Eleanor Robinson":

> *"Every single thing that you do has to be gone through with a fine-toothed comb, and then there are always hurdles to overcome in order to get somewhere, in order to get an outcome. Seeing a matter, you might hear a story, and think, 'That seems so unjust', or 'That seems unfair', but as a lawyer, you can't just look at it as being unfair, you have to look at the law, and what's available at law, and look at something in such a way where you're picking pieces apart, and you're looking to overcome things. I suppose, if you're a pessimist, you're always looking for a challenge, and the fact that something may not work out, and at least, if you have that view, as opposed to a really optimistic, positive view, you're probably applying the law in a better way."*

"Monty" (a junior lawyer in a top-tier Australian commercial law firm, who requested that his name be withheld):

> *"I think that the nature of law is, at least from my experience, that legal guys look for risks – you look to fix people's mistakes; you are cynical and critical – that is your role. The commercial guys are the ones that push the optimism and push for value*

19 Watson and Field, n 10, 395–6.

> *adding and deal making, and lawyers usually are the ones that have to identify any problems with those plans or deals. When it goes bad, they [commercial lawyers] come to us to fix them."*

Sophie Waples (Tipstaff for a Australian state-based Supreme Court Justice):

> *"I think one of the big things with law is that, from the very beginning, we're taught to look for flaws; flaws in legislation, flaws in problems, flaws in contracts. So you're constantly looking, essentially, for the negative things as opposed to pulling out the positive things. I would be reluctant to say that the pessimists, like a general pessimistic outlook on life would outweigh an optimistic outlook on life, but I can see how, in some regards, it might be – you are taught to pull out the flaws in law a lot of the time."*

Much of the research in this area, such as the quotes referenced above, deduce that pessimism is not necessarily a detrimental trait for lawyers to have; rather, it can be virtuous because it affords you the ability to quickly foresee and grasp any potential problems that can arise.[20] This becomes a problem, however, when your personal and professional lives intersect. This crossover allows your work traits to spill into your personal life, and affect who you are as a human being.

Ultimately, regardless of what profession you are in, it can sometimes be difficult to switch off once you have left the office. In the case of a legal professional, maintaining an air of pessimism has worrying connotations. In my opinion, the worrying connotations stem from the level of trust you have in those closest to you, and/or the quantum of satisfaction you receive from a joyful experience.

20 Martin E.P. Seligman, Paul R. Verkuil and Terry H. Kang, "Why Lawyers are Unhappy" (2005) 10 (1) *Cardozo Law Review* 49.

Perfectionism and competitiveness

The *Courting the Blues* report states:

> *"It has been suggested that law education is far more competitive than other forms of tertiary education. Clearly, such competition might work to reduce the level of support that sub-groups of students give each other. Accordingly, competitive elements in an educational setting need to be publicly acknowledged, and supportive mechanisms need to be available for students. Students need to recognise that although their educational experiences may necessitate some level of competition, the competitive element does not need to be incorporated into the personal aspects of their student lives. Students must develop differing skills, which can be used in the professional and personal aspects of their lives. In this regard, legal professionals and students are no different from other professionally-trained people."*[21]

Based on my experiences in law school, and in the law field, I believe it is fair to say that there is an underlying culture that values esteem and prestige, as a determinant of one's worth, among peers. This can materialise in a range of scenarios such as assessment grades, seniority in a club or society, brand recognition of one's employer, salary, and/or a win-loss ratio. Undoubtedly, this is a troubling phenomenon. Law students and young lawyers need to have other, more personal indicators of individual worth, and not be concerned by something as superficial as how much your peers earn. Those indicators should not dictate how you perceive your standing within the law field, or your future as a successful lawyer.

Vines and Tani referred to this phenomenon as a lack of social-connectedness.[22] In fact, these researchers found

21 Kelk et al, n 4.

22 Tani and Vines, n 17.

that this lack of social-connectedness is a prevalent factor in depressive states, especially among law students and young lawyers. The focus on the abovementioned external stimuli gives rise to idiosyncratic ways of perfectionism and competitiveness when managing and manoeuvring one's way through the early years in the law field. People, inside or outside the legal profession, need to be socially connected to one another and well supported during times of distress. Those individuals are then less likely to become depressed in the face of stressful situations. Law students and young lawyers who display high levels of perfectionism and competitiveness tend to develop "high and unrealistic standards, combined with relentless self-criticism",[23] and this can escalate and exacerbate psychological distress, anxiety, and depression.

When asked about these personality types, and any stereotypes that may surface across the board, our interviewees reported the following.

Lauren Fitzpatrick:

> *"A very competitive, high achieving person [is the typical personality type in law]. I think [having those traits] could have a positive effect in that people are constantly striving to achieve their best and work their hardest to be successful, but at the same time, people can put far too much pressure on themselves, and failure to succeed could trigger mental illness."*

Paul Redmond:

> *"There are a number of stereotypes depending on the work you're doing. I think in some kinds of common law and criminal litigation, persons become adversarial. You need a certain level of aggression and assertiveness. Transactional work, where you are trying to anticipate future problems, the predicaments that your client might be in under this transaction or the relationship of the transaction is meant to be documenting, so of course*

23 Ibid.

you're looking always for the worst outcome, so yes, it does favour always a view of what can go wrong rather then building up, as an investment banker might do, the relationship between the parties, promoting it. If you're always worrying about what can go wrong, if you're a professional whose concern is about what might go wrong, of course you tend to see life through lenses that are not rose coloured; in fact, your job is actually to avoid the rose and see the risks, and of course it does make you a glass half empty person, it has a disposition that way."

Jade Tyrrell (a junior lawyer for a mid-tier Australian commercial law firm):

"There is that idealistic, glamorous side of law and then there is the underlying reality of studying law. There are the hard hours that you have to put in. There is reading that you have to do. There are the expectations that lay heavily on your shoulders that you have to meet in order to be the ideal law student, the ideal lawyer. So I think those aspects really came to a head later on in my degree and especially around key periods, such as clerkship applications. I think that is a key time in a student's life where all of a sudden they are expected to be this student who has achieved a distinction average, is ideal in every single way, is completely balanced, has excelled. So in my view we're pushed to this bottleneck of opportunity, or this perceived bottleneck, where if you don't fit the moulds, it's almost like... you are not shunned, but it's almost like you're not the ideal."

Maxine Evers:

"A typical law student or young lawyer is someone who is competitive, someone who is a hard worker, someone who's obviously intelligent, and someone who's committed, and has a commitment to do something. I think that you recognise that you're going to make sure that you give 100 per cent plus to what you're being asked to do. Certainly my experience, both as a practitioner and as an academic, is this kind of competitive edge, feeling that you've got to be the winner, you've got to be on top, you've got to get it right 100 per cent of the time, cannot

be healthy, and certainly cannot be positive."

Danny Gilbert:

"To get into law school, you need to perform strongly in your HSC results and to achieve a high score for university entrance is highly competitive. It produces people who are engaged in the competition. Competition does add stress in people's lives. Some people are equipped to deal with it and some are not. Just because one achieved high university scores and did well at university does not mean a person is temperamentally well-equipped to deal with stress and competitive pressure in the workplace."

Lucinda Clarke:

"Lawyers are generally either naturally perfectionists, or taught to be one, and this mentality is generally an unhealthy one (being a former perfectionist myself, I feel confident to make this judgement). Perfectionism can lead to constant dissatisfaction at work done – even work done very well – and a lack of confidence. Industriousness can lead to a lawyer being stuck late at work because they say that they don't mind staying back, or because they feel working longer hours than their colleagues will serve them well. The desire to please others means lawyers will often say yes to too many things, and this leads to a pattern building, and some being treated like doormats. It also leads to an obvious exhaustion, and a high risk that such a lawyer will burn out.

"Law attracts A-type personalities who tend to be perfectionists, and who are incredibly industrious, who also tend to be people that place a lot of pressure on themselves to excel/succeed. These people tend to already be particularly busy and hard working, but often will still push themselves to always be improving and bettering themselves. This pressure teamed with natural competition from their peer group means that unrealistic expectations are set. This is not so much something I noticed at the university personally (although I know from friends that it did exist), but have definitely noticed

since working in corporate law. There is pressure placed on lawyers to work hard, and attain perfect results, where anyone who can't 'hack' the long hours, and demanding deadlines, and general pressure of the job, is seen as someone who can't cope. This is another unrealistic expectation, which can lead to both distress and anxiety."

"John" (a solicitor working in immigration and refugee law):

"I've barely met a law student that isn't competitive, and who didn't place great stock in doing well. There is a strong level of identification with one's result, and there's this masochistic culture of boasting about the hours one works, and the drudgery one is prepared to endure to get one's hands on the prize. But there is a such a great diversity in forms of legal practice, and types of study that students pursue to get into those forms of legal practice."

Louisa Fitz-Gerald (General Counsel for a public sector legal practice):

"Law attracts people who have very high expectations of themselves, who are perfectionists, and who've always been sort of a big fish in a small pond. You know, they were probably the smartest kids in primary school, and probably high-performing kids in high school, and then they went to the university, and you know, sure, it's all law students in law school, but as compared to the university, they're the ones going to world's debating, or doing mooting, or being in plays, and being in the model of the United Nations. They come out with resumés that would rival 45 year olds, and they're 22 years old. I think the kind of pressure that people put on themselves is really extraordinary, and I think that's part of it."

One of the most interesting things I came across when researching this book was the idea that law students and young lawyers seek and play off motivation that comes from external factors, rather than internal emotions. I noted at the start of this chapter that countering any negative outcomes that emerge, as a result of having certain personality traits, is something that a young legal professional has a greater level of autonomy over, given that those traits are intrinsically based. What is required of you, the reader, is to re-evaluate your perception of that extrinsic stimulus, in order to better manage your responses, emotional health, and psychological wellbeing.

So where do we go from here?

It is important to understand that possessing these idiosyncrasies (i.e. pessimism, perfectionism, and competitiveness) is not always a bad thing, because they can, after all, propel you to personal and professional success. However, if left unchecked, they can also emerge as adverse attributes, which can wreak havoc upon your emotional and psychological wellbeing. The next chapter will offer practical strategies that you can implement into your life to counterbalance pessimism, perfectionism and competitiveness.

Personalities, Part II: Overcoming our legal idiosyncrasies

This chapter outlines the diverse and effective methods employed to combat the quirks that we, as legal professionals, seem to exude. Some of the methods provided may work better for you than others, but it is important to be aware of the different strategies available to you if and when you find yourself vulnerable to traits that can affect your wellbeing.

Learn to be okay with not always being number one

It is extremely important to allow yourself to re-evaluate your perspective, and consider how much stock you should actually place in being the best at every little task and/or assignment. This approach is not always sustainable. It is important to give yourself breathing space, especially if you do not meet the lofty expectations that you set for yourself.

Learning that it is acceptable to fail sometimes was one of the hardest lessons I ever learned, and it was certainly the most humbling. But the insight gained from that first experience of failure has been critical in allowing me to relax in times of exorbitant stress.

Maxine Evers:

> *"Have a rethink about not necessarily being number one, or being the best as the goal, but doing the best that you can do. I think it's about awareness around your personality type, around your approach to the study of law or practice of law."*

Troy Douglas:

> *"People need to be allowed to fail, and be okay with failing. And that's very much a business and commercial thing, as it is in law school. There is so much pressure that you need to succeed, that you have to be first, but sometimes because of where you are in your life, and the fact that you do have other stuff going on, you need to be okay to fail."*

Marie Jepson:

> *"It is possible to reframe your thinking. Instead of 'I have to be the best' in its place substitute 'I will do the best I can'. Experiencing disappointment is part of life and does not equate with failure. Through self-awareness, supportive mentors and friends, an individual can learn to change his perceptions and develop a more realistic and balanced perspective. It allows one to say, 'A poor result in an assignment or exam is not what*

I would like, but it does not define who I am, or mean that I am a failure. My worth as a person is not dependent on the grades I achieve.' In the legal community, choosing to change one's own professional expectations as well as the perceptions of peers is not easy to achieve on one's own. Ongoing support and encouragement make all the difference."

Direct your attention elsewhere, when need be

Lauren Fitzpatrick recommends maintaining activities outside of your study and work that bring you pleasure. This may come across as a form of escapism, and perhaps it is, but involvement in things that sustain your physical, emotional, and intellectual wellbeing are crucial when trying to adapt your personality to the study and practice of law.

"Pull back, I'd say. And not just focus on law. I think the one thing that has been drilled into me is to have things outside your studies, like sport and social life and other jobs or hobbies that aren't necessarily related to your profession so you have areas of escape."

Have outside activities that inspire you

Paul Redmond advocates more altruistic activities, for the reason that they have the ability to remind you of the true purpose of the legal profession, which is to serve the community around it. Therefore, throwing yourself into volunteering can add value to your professional psyche, because it allows you to practise your skills in a practical and helpful forum.

> *"I think the difficulty is to find the time to do things that are life affirming, that are relationship affirming and that are not grounded as worst possible outcomes, the same with cataclysmic outcomes. Picking up work that is personal plight lawyering, volunteering, pro-bono work, to me is a really important and sustaining thing.*
>
> *"I used to be involved in pro-bono in legal aid referral clinics when I was just starting up, later going to Redfern Legal Centre, and for me, that was very satisfying. Acting in this way as part of your professional role as a lawyer gives you a sense of satisfaction, it sustains you through the harder grind through this life-enhancing work."*

It is very important for these activities to not have a competitive or perfectionist element to them. Even social team sports can achieve this, in that you can learn that it is possible to enjoy life without a prize waiting for you at the conclusion. I have discovered this through team sporting activities post-school.

While I still try my best to win, and am thrilled when I do, I no longer mind losing at indoor soccer or mixed netball. The pursuit is enjoyable and fruitful enough as it is, and ultimately I am simply grateful for the opportunity to have fun with my friends.

Manage the expectations of the environment that you are in

Lucinda Clarke advises that one should take the educational and professional environment for what it is, and adapt when necessary. This approach allows you to thrive in that context, rather than fight it. So recognise your skills and knowledge, and utilise them to the best of your ability.

> *"Accept the rigours of the profession, and apply oneself (as best as possible) to the standards expected. This means recognising that your skills will require you to be detail-oriented, thorough, academic, risk-taking, and conservative (and yet commercial!). That is the reality of the job, and the sooner you accept it, the sooner you can enjoy your job, while doing tasks well."*

This can also be achieved through a conscious appreciation for who you are, what your strengths and talents are, and what you have to offer the world. I know that all I can do is be the best possible version of myself, and that way I will be productive and successful, both personally and professionally.

Calm down

Lucinda also offers a second approach, which is simply to calm yourself down. Calming yourself down when you become upset is much easier said than done, but teaching yourself to avoid overreacting is not only helpful personally and emotionally, but it also helps you professionally.

> *"CHILL OUT. That is, remember that there are deadlines and timelines etc., but that the sky won't fall if it is discovered that a court book folder has been tabbed incorrectly, or even something slightly more dramatic. Lawyers tend to get themselves into a flap over nothing, and it is very valuable early on to be the lawyer in the team who refuses to lose their cool and panic or flip out.*
>
> *"Always aim to be the beacon of calm in a sea of flapping lawyers, senior associates, and partners. To do this means that your deadlines will always seem manageable. Plus, you will enjoy your job more."*

Have helpful, practical mentors

James Tobin discusses the importance of having people in your life that can help you, when your competitiveness, perfectionism, and/or pessimism become too overwhelming. Having such mentors and allowing them into your inner circle is crucial because they can offer learned perspectives that you may not have the capacity or foresight to fully understand.

> *"I think it's always very important to have mentors, and to have people who you can talk to. A mentor isn't someone who you necessarily get appointed to. He or she is someone who you have had exposure to, and you trust, and someone who you think can add value to your career. Mentors tend to find you, rather than you finding them, and it's always a good idea to choose someone that is more experienced, or older than you. If you go and talk to one of these mentors – to bounce problems off them, and/or run things by them, it can be very therapeutic, and it can also help you deal with things better."*

Since 2011, I have relied heavily – personally, educationally, emotionally and professionally – on Professor Paul Redmond, whom I came to know when we were joint founders and co-directors of the UTS Brennan Justice and Leadership Program.

This relationship has been tremendously fruitful not only in keeping me grounded and inspired, but also because it has allowed me to develop a close friendship. As far as mentors go, I am very lucky to have had this experience, and I am much richer for it.

Focus on the things you can control, not the things you can't

"Eleanor Robinson" recommends directing your attention towards the things that you have autonomy over, rather than those that are outside of your influence. By redirecting your attention towards more individually focused items, you will ultimately have greater control over your life, health and career.

> *"In terms of being competitive, it's around you, and that's fine, but you are not going to get anywhere, if you get caught up in that. You can only focus on what you have control over, and what you have control over is what you know, and the job you can do, and the tasks you can do."*

I have found that by redirecting your attention and focus away from those things that are outside of your control, you also give yourself a much greater chance of avoiding the need for perfection. This can be a healthy exercise in self-awareness!

Learn to ask questions and seek help, rather than going at it alone

Ashleigh Fehrenbach encourages you to speak out, and request assistance when needed, rather than succumbing to an internal pressure to manage overwhelming tasks alone. And while there is no doubt that some items will require individual attention and customised solutions, you will be better able to follow up with your superior or teacher and get more in-depth details on your current project, so that you can do the best job possible.

> *"I think that you need to be able to ask questions and not just take it upon yourself all the time to find the answer. Whether that's utilising your lecturers or tutors or asking your friends at law school, ask questions and create a discussion so that you don't feel isolated in constantly having to figure everything out for yourself. In terms of the perfectionist aspect, try to recognise that one assignment, one exam is not the be all and end all...I guess it's changing a mindset to getting work completed through a manageable process rather than needing it to be perfect every single time."*

Ashleigh and I both expand upon this idea in the later chapter "How can I manage an often-onerous workload in law?"

Chat regularly with your friends

Anthony Lieu, a graduate lawyer with an online law firm, discusses a simple yet crucial strategy, which is to debrief consistently with your friends. For him, this was a way of gaining critical perspective on the experiences of those around him, to illuminate his own, and gain long-term benefit.

> *"During law school, students are exposed to career paths primarily through their law student body. Commercial firms, creating a skewed impression of what careers are available to law students, often sponsor the promotion of these opportunities. This subsequently results in a certain mindset and culture about career paths upon graduating. However, the reality about career opportunity is much different and the outlook is more positive than it appears.*
>
> *"A law degree is a passport to work in a number of fields, including commercial practice. By bridging the information gap, law students can be more genuine about their career aspirations and pursue a breadth of different opportunity. With an oversupply of law graduates and a tightening job market,*

law students are undoubtedly becoming more stressed about their first job upon graduating. Changing the dialogue in law schools and promoting the plethora of opportunity available for law students is a key step in addressing student wellbeing."

Have connections outside of law that provide different perspectives

Following on from Anthony's point, Luke Furness touches on an issue that I find particularly helpful – the importance of having networks outside of law.

While I adore my lawyer friends, I still maintain close relationships with my non-lawyer friends from school, most of whom have never studied or practised law. These friends have little understanding of the machinations and idiosyncrasies of the legal community, which provides a welcome relief, whenever I see them. They give me perspective on the ways in which I conduct myself and live my life – a perspective that I am not always able to get from my lawyer friends.

Luke Furness:

"I think the first and foremost thing is to have friends and experiences outside of the law field, because if the studies are true, and pessimists survive more in law, then by definition, people in other fields, such as optimists are like, 'Don't worry about it' types of people, and so, if you surround yourself with those types of people on the weekends, suddenly it all becomes a lot easier to deal with. For instance, you can say, 'My partner yelled at me for a typo.' It may be serious to you when you are a 'Type-A personality' but your friends just say, 'Don't worry about that, let's focus on something positive, let's go out on Saturday night.'

"I think that's the best strategy. And it is probably an opposite strategy, in which talking to other people about what

> *you're going through – what you are going through at the firm, really trying to be as cooperative as you can with the grads, and chatting with them because you can guarantee they are going through the same things. They may not always tell you, because they feel that there's a little bit of competition sometimes. So there is no pride in showing weakness, but if you can break down those walls, as soon as possible, I think the empathy will really help you."*

Speaking to someone who has a different way of viewing the world, and appreciating their point of view, doesn't mean that your way is wrong or that they are right. But it does mean that you may not be so tied to pessimistic opinions, in light of viewpoints to the contrary.

Focus on the client, not the politics

"Peter", a senior lawyer in a mid-tier Australian commercial law firm, also discusses navigating your way through the legal profession, and the metaphorical progression up the ladder. He feels that the competitive nature of lawyers can lead some to put too much stock in their positions within law firms, which can potentially influence their levels of self-worth. This same scenario could play out in the case of a law student who does not get offered the internship or job that he or she desperately wanted. As a result, this individual sees himself or herself as being less intelligent or capable as compared to his or her peers. "Peter" offers a different perspective on the topic – one that will not only change your mindset and encourage you to think more positively, but also improve the way you conduct yourself as a lawyer.

> *"Make the game, and the competition about yourself, not about the people around you, because everyone has different*

ways of doing things, and everyone's got different things that they want out of their careers. Some people will be in it just to become a partner, so, it will be all about office politics and that type of nonsense. If you want to get involved in that, go ahead, but that is going to cause you some grief, I think. If you are in the law field to be a good lawyer, and the best lawyer you can be, then that's when you have to start saying, 'What can I do to be a good lawyer?' It's not by playing office politics, or saying, 'I hope I get to be a partner by 30.'

"Rather, it's by saying that you look forward to providing a service for your clients – recognising that they have come to you for advice, to look after their problems, and with the belief that you will do all of those things in the best way possible. And I think that once you do that, it flows on to other things. I mean, if you are servicing a client well that brings the firm more work. And if the firm gets more work, then you start to get recognised for bringing in work for the firm, then those other things will follow. Now, that may not happen as quickly to someone who knows how to play the game, and make friends with the national managing partner, but it will probably come eventually. And even if it doesn't, as long you enjoy your work, and do a good job every day – you will be happier."

TWD Wellbeing Wisdom

Listed below is a summary of what was discussed in this chapter:

- When necessary, allow yourself to be okay with not always being number one. Be okay with occasional failure, if and when it happens. It does not reflect on you as a person or a professional.
- Pursue interests outside of the law, and add value to your personal and professional development by taking an in-depth look at your life (perspective).
- Accept the legal environment around you for what it is, and adapt your approach to best suit that environment.
- Relax your approach to legal tasks, and avoid overreacting to those tasks.
- Seek useful and practical mentors to guide you through your vocational journey.
- Narrow your focus to those things that you can control, and discard the ones you cannot.
- Remember that is it okay to ask questions, and request assistance, if needed.
- Develop non-legal networks, so you can retain a holistic perspective on life, and your place in it.
- Avoid playing office politics – be yourself; be the best legal professional you can be.

Dr Fisher offered comments in response to being told of these solutions listed above, in professing a medical perspective.

> *"These statements above reflect a mature attitude to establishing a balanced life, one part of which is the individual's professional occupation.*
>
> *"A mature person would look at this advice and say, 'Well, of course that's of course how we should operate.'"*

ALSA supports my findings as well as the comments of Dr Fisher.

"Law students and young legal professionals need to adopt one simple mentality: Don't see someone else's success as your failure. Once this mentality is adopted and understood, some of the anxieties and pressures of studying law slowly dissipate. We encourage students to focus on their own success and to remember that success is not a straight trajectory line, but rather involves many peaks and troughs. Law students and lawyers should always be reminded that some of our greatest successes would not be possible without failing, that failure is not final and that learning from failure is a success in itself. We also encourage a greater sense of collegiality among law students and young lawyers: while ruthless competition can lead to some success, it is also likely to burn bridges and leave you feeling rather lonely. We believe that success is far more rewarding and satisfying when relationships have been built in the process."

There is nothing wrong with the personality traits that you possess. They have led you onto the path of exploring law, as an educational and vocational pursuit, and that is to be applauded. If and when those personality traits interfere with your wellbeing, then it becomes necessary to learn how to effectively manage them.

How can law teachings and practices affect our wellbeing?

An increasingly important issue (and one that I find particularly curious) is how technological advancements have exacerbated the propensity for lawyers to work extraordinary hours, given that they now have around-the-clock access to legal matters. In fact, a number of my graduate lawyer friends feel the need to give out their work email addresses and mobile phone numbers to clients and colleagues so as to be accessible at all times, in exchange for an employer-paid monthly phone bill (partially or completely).

And while the idea of such access may seem practical in work terms, or even exciting for a graduate lawyer, it can also trigger a situation in which the lawyer cannot reasonably "switch off" from work materials (literally and metaphorically). This prevents the lawyer from having a physical separation from life at the office. This disturbing trend is the reason why people can no longer press the "off" button on their work lives[24] and, as a result, lawyers are allowing themselves less time to rejuvenate (or recharge the batteries, as I like to say), which ultimately creates long-term negative consequences on their emotional and psychological wellbeing.

In addition, certain teachings and learning methodologies have the effect of rendering law students as passive, uncritical cogs in the legal machine. Therefore, because of these methods, such as a 100 per cent exam, the real interests of law students are repressed, because they cannot properly have a critical discussion on the social and legal status quo. This lack of critical discussion results in the development of cynical attitudes regarding the ability of law to effect meaningful societal change, and the loss of idealism (concerning law and its place in the world).[25]

As mentioned before, the study and practice of law is not for everyone. Some people are more suited to the academic, technical or administrative professional rigours that law offers, whereas others perceive law as an industry founded on theatrical courtroom monologues, and are then let down when this is revealed to be mythical.

But this doesn't mean that those who choose to study and practise law shouldn't continue to pursue it; rather, they should find an avenue through which legal education and experience can best suit their academic prowess and career ambition. In addition, law students and young lawyers should manage their expectations about what the legal profession can and will offer them; utilise the study and practice of law for

---

24 Leanne Mezrani, "Lawyers Need More Time To Do Their Job", *Lawyers Weekly* (online) 19 February 2015 <http://www.lawyersweekly.com.au/news/16186-lawyers-need-more-time-to-do-their-job?utm_source=lawyersweekly&utm_campaign=lawyersweekly_Bulletin19_02_2015&utm_medium=email>

25 Matthew Ball, "Legal Education and the 'Idealistic Student': Using Foucault to unpack the critical legal narrative" (2010) 36 (2) *Monash University Law Review* 80.

what it is, so that they can achieve their personal goals, rather than those supposedly dictated by the hypothetical masses.

This chapter will examine the experiences of current and former law students, along with current lawyers, and how they adapt to the teachings and methodological styles of law schools and legal practices. It will also examine how these experiences can affect educational and professional developments, along with emotional and psychological wellbeing. Lastly, this chapter will explore how to thrive in such an environment.

Any attempts to prevent or counter mental health problems must be simultaneously met with a shift in cultural attitudes towards mental health conditions like depression and anxiety. For example, when introducing measures to provide pastoral care to law students, universities must ensure that those measures are performed in a manner that is private, supportive and engages the entire on-campus community.

Two senior lecturers and barristers from the University of Newcastle noted that:

> *"...If lawyers suffer clinical depression significantly more than the general population, many would think that law schools should reconsider their curriculum."*[26]

This is true to the extent that given the startling frequency of depression among law students, universities can, and should attempt to take greater care of its students. There are a number of ways that law schools can attempt to achieve this.

26 James and Finlay-Jones, n 14, 32.

Adopt a refocused approach on students' thought processes

The study and practice of law is a "black letter" discipline. Laws have affected so much of society's day-to-day order and efficiency that it has retained this singular disposition. In fact, one of the first lessons law students learn is that unless you are asked to examine the philosophical or historical aspects of law, there is little scope for imagination or creativity in writing about legal matters.

This can be disenchanting and limiting for high school graduates and post-graduate art majors who are fluent in Shakespearean eloquence, romanticism, and philosophical theory; in some cases, delving into the study and practice of law can be quite perplexing. If educational, vocational, and existential confusion develops, mental health conditions may arise.

As mentioned previously, the study and practice of law is not for everyone. Some people are more suited to the academic and professional rigours of law than others.

The discipline of law often appears to be taught in a way that suppresses a student's ability to think and reason in a moral or experiential sense. Law school teaches you to think in rational terms, which can have the tendency to spill over into one's personal life, as opposed to simply remaining in the educational or professional spheres of one's existence.

Lawrence Krieger, a clinical professor and outspoken critic of the supposedly narrowly focused legal education that purports to nurture students (with the intellectual inclination to "think like a lawyer") argues:

> *"'Thinking like a lawyer' is fundamentally negative; it is critical, pessimistic, and depersonalising. It is a damaging paradigm in law schools because it is usually conveyed, and understood, as a new and superior way of thinking, rather than an important,*

but strictly limited legal tool."[27]

Why are the consequences of this educational method so worrying? Well, because the ability to think and reason with morality and emotion resonates with the capacity to maintain empathy, humour, and social connections. These traits are critical to the psychological wellbeing of students in the midst of a highly competitive and rigorous academic program.[28] Being able to separate law school from everyday life is a fundamentally important skill, so as to avoid psychological distress and anxiety. I agree with Krieger's assertions that in adopting such clinical and rational approaches to these areas of life that are unrelated to legal studies or the practice of law, a student's emotional wellbeing can be severely affected.

I am not proposing that those who choose to study and practise law should not continue to pursue it; rather, I believe that these individuals should find an avenue that accentuates their education and experiences. These individuals should use their knowledge and expertise to fuel their career pursuits. In addition, these students and young lawyers should have realistic expectations on what the legal profession can and will offer them.

Utilise the study and practice of law for what it is, and you will achieve your personal goals. Do not get bogged down by goals that are dictated by the masses. Also, being able to think and reason clearly, or at least accurately distinguish between the thought processes of both the legal and non-legal career sectors, is crucial to retaining your "sense of self".

---

27 Lawrence S. Krieger, "What we're not telling law students, and lawyers, that they really need to know: some thoughts-in-action towards revitalising the profession from its roots" (1998) 13 *Journal of Law and Health* 1.

28 Kath Hall, Molly Townes O'Brien and Stephen Tang, "Developing a Professional Identity in Law School: A View from Australia" (2010) 4 *Phoenix Law Review* 19.

Overly demanding assessments in law school

According to the 2011 text, *The Mental Health Supplement* (which served as the 2009 addendum to the handbook, *Depression in Law Schools*), the Australian Law Students' Association printed a story from a law student attending Griffith University (Gold Coast). The student, whom I choose not to name, wrote:

> *"We raised an issue with our university over our 24-hour take-home exam for the core subject of Constitutional Law. The assessment was to take place during study week or exam week. This became an issue because many students, over the past three years, had been complaining about the stress that it caused them – many of whom did not sleep for the entire 24-hour period, and this affected their ability to study for other exams. After learning about the link between stress and depression, and the effects it may have on the learning experience of students, we thought it would be a good issue to raise with our law school. They were initially surprised by our concerns, but they were also really interested in what we had to say, and the argument we put forth. We highlighted our concerns over the lack of sleep, and stress that students are faced with, at that time of year, as well as the fact that other law schools had similar concerns and views on this issue. Luckily, the law school reacted positively. There are always going to be some students, who 'like' assessments such as: 100 per cent finals or 24-hour take-home exams. However, it may not necessarily be the best practice for their and their fellow students' mental health."*[29]

29 Australian Law Students' Association, *Mental Health Supplement* 25 <www.alsa.net.au/images/2011/2011_ALSA_Mental_Health.pdf>

An expected and common practice among legal educators, particularly those involved with the practical legal training of law students, is to immerse students in the practices of the legal profession for the purposes of equipping them for any rigours and challenges that their future careers may present, for example, "all-nighters", in which lawyers may work around the clock to meet client or court deadlines.

In my mind, however, this is exponentially outweighed by the need to ensure the wellbeing of students. The notion that a university can, or even should, prepare students for a career in law by compelling them to undergo arduous assessments, which can potentially have adverse effects on their health and wellbeing is utterly ridiculous. Not only does this fail my interpretation of the duty of care that a faculty has to its students, it can also be seen as a succumbing to a perception of the legal profession as being overly rigorous, notwithstanding that this environment will probably not be encountered by a significant number of law graduates who choose to go down different career paths.

Is legal work too negatively geared?

It is sometimes difficult to counter the perception that legal work is adversarial, dispute-oriented, and subsequently negatively geared. This may be deemed a limited view. However, depending on the area, it can also be seen as a reasonable depiction of the nature and practice of law.

"Eleanor Robinson":

> *"...People don't come to us because they're happy. Our clients, at public sector legal services, come to us because they're in trouble, or are criminals, and if you think about family law, they're coming to you because they're going through a divorce.*

> *Even contractual law, all this dealing with huge amounts of money, they're not coming to you because they're happy, they're coming because they've got some real concerns, and you're dealing with it, you're the person on the end of it, and we don't have training in how to deal with crazy clients or difficult clients, we're just here, we're told that we're lawyers, and we can't help them any other way than doing our jobs. It's a world made and built on anxiety."*

Regardless of your daily practices, this can have a significant impact upon the ways in which a legal professional may view the world around him or her. As emotional beings, we have the ability to empathise with other people's feelings and situations, which, in some cases, is quite difficult to manage and navigate.

Maxine Evers:

> *"Sometimes it's hard not to be brushed with the client's emotions. Even though as a lawyer we know that we must be professionally detached from clients' problems, it is very difficult to turn off when you leave the office, and then switch back into lawyer mode when you come back in the next morning. I think that's also because you are spending so much time at work that the majority of your own time is absorbed with various clients' concerns and problems."*

Because of this, it becomes all the more important for you to be able to disconnect once you walk out the door of your office, and return to the real world. This does not mean that you should escape from your job. To suggest as much implies that your job is something that you need escaping *from*. What I am saying is that you need other things in your life that provide emotional and intellectual stimulation, so the bulk of your energy does not fixate on whatever is happening at your job. Having a balance between work and your outside life is all-important because a work/life balance is crucial to health and wellbeing.

This topic will be explored in greater detail in the chapter,

What is the best way for me to achieve a work-life balance?

Allow yourself personal space and time

It is also important to give yourself time to rest and unwind. According to Marie Jepson, allowing oneself to enjoy life away from work is a foreign concept to many lawyers.

> *"Long working hours, delaying gratification and prioritising work commitments over family, friends, holidays, passions leave little time for balance and positive experiences. Over time this negativity can become a 'slippery slope' leading to depression."*

This practice of sidelining enjoyable events and activities is something that I have been guilty of in the past, and it is something that I subsequently would never recommend to anyone else. By allowing myself to believe that nothing was more important than my work, study, and what I was trying to achieve professionally in my life, I got to a point where having fun almost felt like a sin. This is no way to go about your life.

Law does not have to be your life – so don't let it take over

The next point focuses on ensuring that you have a life outside of law. In my interview with "Grace" – an in-house legal counsel who wished to remain anonymous – she touched on a scenario which I have witnessed countless times since entering law school and the legal profession (and have, in all likelihood, been an active player in). This discussion involves making law a regular topic of conversation, if not a dominating one.

> *"I saw some colleagues on my way home one night, and they started talking to me about work at the firm, and the way that they were speaking caused me to pretend that I was really cold. So I went inside of the ferry because I couldn't stand listening to them being so negative and hearing all the horrible things that were happening at the firm. It caused me to suddenly get anxious about going back to work. And, as a result, I couldn't stand talking to them."*

Given the long hours of study and practice, it is perhaps inevitable or even understandable that law can consume your conscious being to the extent that nothing else warrants discussion. However, this moves you in the opposite direction from being able to completely separate (emotionally and physically) from work. While telling a fib to escape a conversation might not be the most ideal solution, the principle should remain the same – if you feel the need to distance your personal and professional existences – take steps to ensure that they are kept separate!

One does not have to engage in legally influenced discussions when one is not at the office, however, it can also be more difficult to prevent legal thoughts and processes from influencing your psyche. Aimee Riley, for example, notes how her legal training and experience sometimes dictates how she approaches life tasks and relationships.

> *"I find that [the culture] translates into how I am in my personal life. My work experiences where I have seen other people's negative situations play out, makes me less trusting and more controlling over my own personal life. For example, I wouldn't trust my boyfriend to go and enter into a contract that also binds me without being actively involved in the process. I am also obsessed with knowing the granular detail of things and details being accurate. I think law school produces a very highly analytical but critical perspective on people and life, and also*

> *a very different internal perspective because I'm constantly looking at what I'm doing that's not ideal. I'm looking at all the mistakes I've made rather than all the good things I've done."*

In the context of buying a house or car, allowing your legal knowledge and skills to influence your responses can be the difference between a good and bad deal. However, it is crucial that you do not let this seep into more intimate aspects of your being, such as developing a distrust of those closest to you.

Note: This is not what happened in Aimee's case, but hypothetically, it would not be fruitful for you to allow critical analysis and reasoning to dictate the nature of your personal relationships, because it is important to ensure that you have a network of friends and family who are not connected to your law world. Having people close to you with diverse opinions, values, skills, and hobbies not only provides you with a broader perspective on your own personal and professional life, it also gives you that separation you sometimes need. Luke Furness points out the danger of not having such a diverse network.

> *"You should not always be interacting with people from work in a solid critical way, but I think in life we are trained to do it at work, and we might be trained to do it in all areas of work, and sometimes even in home situations, so, if that is solely what we are doing, yeah, that could potentially be damaging."*

Internal influences on the legal environment

Thus far, this chapter has focused on external factors that can affect an individual, but there are also certain internal and/or self-induced factors that can also affect a person's wellbeing when studying or practising law. Moreover, it has been established that law students and young lawyers typically put an immense amount of pressure on themselves to perform at high levels (with goals that are to be achieved at frantic paces).

"Fraser", a junior lawyer in a top-tier Australian commercial law firm, has witnessed this.

> *"I do see that in my firm, there's a lot of pressure placed on the individuals to perform, to make deadlines, and there is no option to seek an extension, or anything like that, so sometimes there's not enough bodies to get work done in a stable way. I don't know what the causes are – whether it's a chicken or an egg, whether it attracts people who are perfectionistic, pessimistic, highly motivated and driven, causing them to perform unacceptably (not meeting pre-set standards). You need to realign how you perceive yourself and recognise that just because something didn't go right it doesn't mean that you've failed yourself, rather it just means that you dealing with it, or that it is purely the environment that drives people to those extremes."*

Gavin Ingram, the general counsel for an international legal practice, also supports this notion by exploring how this subsequently affects one's ability to achieve a healthy balance in his or her daily life.

> *"There's a lot of pressure to perform – there's always tight deadlines, something's always due yesterday, you're always competing against someone else, your performance today is only as good as what it was yesterday; so it is very competitive. You're so focused on work, on billing, on your output that often, young lawyers neglect themselves, which is a great shame. It's often very hard to get that balance right where you are looking after yourself and also looking after the interests of your client [and the firm]. As you compete with other lawyers, your differential often comes down to your preparedness to sacrifice and make work your number one priority."*

It is, of course, fundamentally important for professional success and productivity to have consideration for those around you, and to do your best for your clients and employers. But such consideration should not be at the expense of your own self. As the old adage states, if you cannot look after yourself, you won't be able to look after anyone else.

Perceived lack of autonomy

Exacerbating this issue of addressing client needs and workplace demands is a perceived lack of autonomy that you have in the earlier years of legal practice. This lack of independence is something that all junior lawyers experience at some point (albeit to different degrees). The impact from it affects how they perceive their self-worth in the workplace, which is an unhealthy mindset to have during those earlier years in the legal profession. Louisa Fitz-Gerald discusses how a lack of autonomy can affect you once you enter the workforce.

> *"When you get into a law firm, you may have absolutely no autonomy. You won't even have autonomy to say, 'Next Wednesday night, I'm going to book a dinner with my friends at 8.30pm.' Why? Well, because you have no idea whether you're going to get out at 8.30pm or not. You have no autonomy to say, 'I don't really like this too much, so I'd rather focus on this…' You're on a task and that's it; you have no decision-making power.*
>
> *"So things last for a long time, and it's very difficult to see light at the end of the tunnel. You don't have any control over what's happening, especially in those early years, unless you're lucky. I think that that's a rude shock when you've come from a position of being able to achieve a lot of short-term things, and being autonomous in the activities that you're doing."*

Another issue to consider on this front is the practice of billing for client services. This isn't a practice that is unique to law, however it could potentially impact upon how much autonomy you may perceive or even have in your daily work. Graeme Cowan has conducted research on this front.

> *"The vast majority of law firms are on time-based billing. All the evidence shows that it is not healthy; it's measuring input and time in rather than effectiveness. Research into motivation says that people want to be involved in mastery, and mastery means you focus on outcomes, outputs, rather than inputs."*

This was supported by the findings of Krieger and Sheldon in their research into the causes of happiness and wellbeing for lawyers:

> *"The specific practice factor that had the strongest negative relationship with wellbeing was required billable hours. This practice was associated with increasing income but decreasing autonomy, relatedness, and internal motivation, an apparent example of managers undermining workers' self-determined motivation and wellbeing by promoting a focus on external rewards. Thus, as billable hours go up, income goes up and happiness goes down."*[30]

The practice of billing is something that will likely, if not definitely, be outside of your control as a professional factor. But that doesn't mean you shouldn't be aware of it and ways in which you can counter potential emotional and psychological effects upon your person.

30 Krieger and Sheldon, n 2, 615.

Law vs. The Rest of the World

At this point in the chapter, I find it apt to compare law to other professions. Paul Redmond, a former dean at one of Australia's biggest law schools, submitted an analogy between law and medicine that drives home the intensity and pressure that often accompanies the study and practice of law.

> *"The nature of the work requires fine detail, focus on detail, avoidance of error, a management of risk; these are all negative qualities and stress-inducing, there's an element of adversarial work, even in transactional law. And I think it's not in many ways affirming of the whole person. Compare law to, say, medicine – in medicine, everybody's on the same team, on the same side, a single team confronting and challenging and working against the conditions that the patient has. In law, people are divided against each other, it's adversarial. Even in transactional work, you always have to frame the contest to be avoided, you know, in adversarial terms. It's not a win-win situation; it's honestly a zero-sum in many cases. And lawyers are there to think always of the worst outcome, and to protect against it, and that isn't the life-affirming, wholesome activity that advertising, marketing or medicine is."*

TWD Wellbeing Wisdom

Patrick Schiltz wrote:

> *"...Lawyers don't see their lives as crazy. Lawyers don't see any of this. Lawyers don't sit down and think logically about why they are leading the lives they are leading any more than buffalo sit down and think logically about why they are stampeding."*[31]

It is important to maintain a holistic approach to the study and practice of law; that is, a resilient lawyer is one who can see beyond the black-letter law, and whose understanding of self, ethical, and societal problems is well-developed.[32] This broader appreciation for law and its place in society can therefore aid one's wellbeing.

If you ever have had a negative reaction to the teachings and methodological practices of law school, and/or legal practice, try bearing in mind the following things:

- The work you are doing has a larger purpose that supersedes any trivial things you encounter. Regardless of whether you are completing a business merger, or defending an accused criminal, there are significant societal and/or business implications that must be considered in the legal field. Therefore, your work efforts are important!
- You are not your client, and therefore, their problems are not your problems. Maintain your perspective and separate your personal and professional lives whenever you feel that those two areas are overlapping.
- Utilising professional skills and knowledge in your personal life can be beneficial, but also detrimental. Any aspect of your study and

31 Patrick J. Schiltz, "On Being a Happy, Healthy and Ethical Member of an Unhappy, Unhealthy and Unethical Profession" (1999) 52 *Vanderbilt Law Review* 905.

32 Prue E. Vines, "Working Towards the Resilient Lawyer: Early Law School Strategies" (Research Paper No. 30, University of New South Wales, 2 July 2011).

practice of law that has the potential to affect you negatively (such as looking for flaws or seeing the worst-case scenario) may need to be left in the office or on-campus!

- There may be occasions where you do not have as much autonomy over a piece of work as you would like. This is par for the course as a junior legal professional. If it gets to a point, however, where practising law in this way affects your wellbeing, then you need to speak to someone.
- If you are consumed by your mobile phone, as I often am, set usage rules for yourself. Force yourself to "switch off" by leaving your mobile phone in the other room, or by only accessing it during certain hours of the day. Even forced separation can be beneficial!

This is supported by comments from Dr Fisher, who offered his thoughts in conjunction with what he perceives to be a mature, civilised human being.

> *"The starting point has to be how you view the world and how you treat yourself. A grown-up person will say, 'Okay, I can go into the law. But what does that mean to me? Does it mean 80-hour weeks? Does it mean I end up getting drunk and using cocaine when I'm exhausted? Does it mean using stimulants in the morning and sleeping tablets in the evening to keep going?'*
>
> *"If a lawyer comes to me in trouble, depressed and anxious, often enough with an established pattern of drug and alcohol abuse, I will encourage them to conduct a stocktake of their life as it is at the present time. I encourage them to consider what is a good life for them.*
>
> *"Freud considered that a good life 'is the balance between self and others and balance between work, relationships and leisure'.*
>
> *"To achieve and maintain such a state of equanimity requires that you obtain enough sleep, eat well enough, and engage in regular exercise. The living of a professional and non-professional life requires effective juggling and prioritisation. These choices need to be informed by a basic philosophy."*

The importance of taking individual responsibility

Over the past ten years, our profession has sought to raise awareness of psychological distress, anxiety, and depression within the legal field. In fact, the emergence of the Tristan Jepson Memorial Foundation (TJMF) has been paramount in achieving this directive, particularly in its delivery of the *Resilience@Law* DVD, a collaborative exploration by five of the biggest law firms in Australia of the topic of depression in law.

In addition, the TJMF *Best Practice Guidelines* was released to help establish a series of workplace standards that purport to improve the psychological wellbeing of individuals and communities within the legal profession. As of February 2015, almost 90 legal institutions around Australia, plus at least one globally, had become signatories to the guidelines – with this number expected to grow. In addition to this, many law firms, law societies and law faculties, nationwide, have implemented their own programs to encourage a healthy work/life balance. Some of these initiatives include external sporting competitions, in-house massages, yoga classes, subsidised boot camps, among many other options.

With all of these initiatives in place, with the profession seemingly looking out for the best interests of law students and lawyers – why then should we take further actions on an individual level, and ensure the wellbeing of others?

There are a variety of reasons why everyone should take individual responsibility for their own actions.

Firstly, not every law student or young lawyer participates in the activities offered by their institution. Two, these activities may not adequately address your own unique personal, emotional, and/or psychological needs. Other strategies and methods may be required to maintain your health and wellbeing. Three, the activities offered at your institution may not adequately suit your schedule, meaning that you may never get to experience those initiatives to the best of your ability.

Additionally, it is becoming quite clear that most employers are not taking the mental health of their lawyers seriously enough. In January 2015, *Lawyers Weekly* published a national survey, conducted by the University of New South Wales, on the importance of mental health and wellbeing in the law field:

> *"...Considerable cynicism among lawyers, regarding mental health and wellbeing programs, with many respondents questioning whether these initiatives are capable of tackling*

systemic issues of stress, depression, and anxiety."[33]

Such programs that are implemented by your employer, or, in the case of a law student, your university or local law society, may indeed work for you. However, it is fair to say that you have a much greater chance of ensuring your own mental health by taking charge of it, than by patiently waiting for the legal profession to give you a helping hand. By taking individual responsibility for your own actions, you shape the management of your health and wellbeing in a manner that best suits your interests, schedule, and motivation.

This chapter focuses on answering the question, "Who ultimately has the obligation, and therefore the power, to nurture your own state-of-being?" I am not suggesting that you bear the burden alone; rather, I am calling for action from everyone. Law students and young lawyers need to take control and responsibility for their own mental health, while in law school, and then while practising law.

One thing I am extremely proud of in discussing my recovery is the fact that I didn't take my illness lying down – I did as much as I could to fight it. Of course, there were moments when I was too fragile, weepy or disenchanted to even get out of bed, let alone seize the day. And there were times when I felt so helpless that I openly expressed complete despair, when perhaps I shouldn't have felt the need to. But by and large, I tried to take charge. By owning the situation, I was able to exercise a greater level of autonomy over my thoughts and feelings than perhaps I otherwise would have been able to.

You, too, can do this.

33 Leanne Mezrani, "You don't really give a damn about our mental health", *Lawyers Weekly* (online) 20 January 2015 <http://www.lawyersweekly.com.au/news/16068-you-don-t-really-give-a-damn-about-our-mental-health>

What it means to look after yourself

I asked interviewees two questions in relation to this issue:

- Where does the responsibility of mental health ultimately lie; and
- When is the best time for law students and young lawyers to assume individual responsibility for themselves, on top of what is being offered by the profession?

A substantial number of interviewees responded that they believed each individual has a duty to himself or herself, first and foremost, to address mental health issues, and ensure their own health and wellbeing.

Don't get me wrong – these responses do not negate the obligation that others (law school communities, legal profession, etc.) have to you, as an individual; rather it simply recognises that, as the proverbial master of your own destiny, you should also take charge of the situation, instead of simply sitting around waiting for assistance.

In recent times, law schools around Australia have started including the idea of personal responsibility and self-management as identifiable learning thresholds and standards by which students can measure their educational development throughout their law degree. Professor Jill McKeough, who also formerly chaired the Council of Australian Law Deans, discussed this further:

> *"Self-management is one of the learning threshold outcomes that has, only in the last five years, been recognised as something that law students should know about. Law schools require students to have this as part of a group of attributes that is going to help them if they need it."*

A prime example of this is in how a law student will undertake the study of their degree. Professor McKeough continues:

> *"I think it's very clear that working very long hours is bad for people and it's quite difficult to maintain a healthy lifestyle with very long hours of work. There's a lot of competition at law school, but on the whole, the program of study is designed so that people can realistically get through. However, if you stress yourself and take on extra study, then that's a matter of self-management that you need to learn. I have noticed that students have an urge to get out as soon as possible and get to work. I think people would do well to realise that taking an extra year is not the end of the world."*

In hindsight, I am thankful that I made the decision to stretch out my law degree by another six months, when I was enrolling for subjects in 2011. At that point, the crippling weight of my schedule was such that I couldn't manage a full-time study load for the autumn semester, and thus decided to push some study units into 2012. Studying for another six months was not a huge deal, especially when one considers that we have to work for approximately 40 or 50 years in our lifetime anyway!

Being proactive about my schedule, and better managing my workload, was a necessary step. It is possible for you to do the same in consideration of your health and wellbeing; being autonomous is not only achievable, but it can be so beneficial for you too.

Lucinda Clarke identified the importance of resilience in taking control over your own situation.

> *"Everyone has to handle his or her own situation to some extent. An optimistic, positive approach teamed with the maintenance of a healthy physical lifestyle is very important. But overall, resilience is the key skill to develop. In my mind, resilience – not happiness – is the opposite of depression. It is very important to develop resilience, and law firms are quite good for this, but*

it is also important to ask for help, and not to suffer in silence."

And Nick Edwards stressed the importance of recognising that no one is better placed than yourself to manage your own affairs, which reinforces my original argument.

> *"The bottom line is your health. At the end of the day that's your responsibility, and no one knows you better than yourself. People have different capacities to handle stress, or anxiety, or problems throughout their lives, and the best person that knows that is the person that stares back at you in the mirror."*

"Adelaide", a junior lawyer in a top-tier Australian commercial law firm, also discussed the necessity to develop an internal drive to improve your wellbeing, whether it is before or after you experienced health problems, because such intrinsic motivation puts you in good stead to manage any issues that arise.

> *"I think that personal responsibility is important. I think there has to be, in everyone's recovery from mental illness, some personal drive even, if there is no motivation...but a mere desire to get better is necessary. Law firms are going to have programs, but law firms are law firms. They are not there to counsel staff members through emotional trauma, and although that sounds really hard, that's what psychological practices are there to do.*
>
> *"That's why they have the employee assistance programs and that sort of stuff, but my view is that I don't think those programs alone are going to help get someone out of a really dark space."*

Matthew Littlejohn also pointed out the numerous avenues of assistance that are readily available to people in need of mental health assistance.

> *"I think it is no longer acceptable for young lawyers to do nothing. Given the amount of education that has been around in the last five years or so, I think that everybody now has a responsibility to be doing something. Go to a program if there's one at your law school or workplace. If there isn't something available, then*

you have to go and find something that you can do for yourself."

It is important to at least bear in mind what Matthew and Sarah Beth (below) advocate, which is to be proactive in acknowledging what is available for you, if and when you require such resources.

> *"Being proactive about supporting yourself means increasing your awareness and searching holistically for programs and networks which work best for you – many are offered in a variety of formats, including online, in person, or over the phone. Utilising the resources available, including those offered by related institutions, referral programs as well as those which might be offered in the workplace, can be really helpful."*

As mentioned, the argument that individual responsibility is crucial does not ignore the fact that your employer or institution has a duty of care to ensure your health and wellbeing – because they absolutely do! And it is imperative that they take that duty seriously. Moreover, "Robert James" believes that it is fundamentally important that an individual is able to springboard into a position whereby he or she feels capable of taking care of himself or herself, and/or those around him or her.

> *"Personal responsibility is, I think, the cornerstone of being successful in law. But, at the same time, one needs to look after one's neighbour. So both really go hand in hand. As much as a person should be proactive in looking after his or her own physical wellbeing, so should the environment, in which he or she studies or works. It's really a combination of individual and social responsibility."*

But how can an individual take responsibility for themselves, and their health, if he or she does not know where to turn? This is a conundrum that countless law students and young lawyers face as they do not feel adequate support is offered.

"Eleanor Robinson":

> *"I've thought a couple of times, where can I actually go to get some help – I am feeling overwhelmed about work. I am someone who is knowledgeable about what is out there, in terms of services, and I don't know what is out there for a young lawyer who doesn't know where to turn. I personally don't know where to turn, so I think they definitely need to do more."*

"Sunrise" was more pointed in her assessment of the situation:

> *"There's all this talk about law students and mental health, and it's good to talk about it, but you also need to give me a way to help myself. It's being discussed, but I don't feel any institution has actually given their students a way to counter these problems. Talking is great, dialogue is good, and it's empowering, but I'm doing two law subjects each semester, and for one of them I need to attend all the tutorials, unless I have a medical certificate, otherwise I lose marks.*
>
> *"One day recently, I had actually thrown up, I just did not want to get out of bed, I was tired, I was stressed, I was crying, I had my own stuff going on in life; I just did not want to get out of bed, and go to the university, and I couldn't go to the doctor, and get a medical certificate, because I was sad, and didn't want to go to the university, and I felt like, if I didn't have that medical certificate, I was going to miss out on marks. But I didn't have the nerve to email my tutor and say, 'I'm feeling really s*** and I don't want to come into class. Can you please excuse my absence from the tutorial?' I felt like my tutor would say, 'Get your s*** together, get your life together, we all have bad days.' I feel that if someone's feeling down, if someone's got depression, they can't miss a day of work…that you can't call in sick with depression or anxiety."*

There have certainly been times when I have felt like "Eleanor Robinson" and didn't know where to turn. And I'd be lying if I said that I'd never had the same experience as "Sunrise" when she said she was reluctant to call in sick out of fear that it would negatively affect her academic or professional evaluations and/or success.

In fairness, it can be difficult to pep yourself up to take individual responsibility for your own actions. And, rightly or wrongly, there is a perception among some young legal professionals that the institution needs to facilitate a greater level of support for its students and lawyers. Such facilitation of support can, in turn, help individuals take charge for themselves in the manner that they ultimately should. Senthorun Raj touches on this.

> *"I think creating networks where lawyers can support each other, or people working in the law can support each other, even if they're not 'lawyers', is essential to that process. Learning about mental health issues does require you to step up and to engage with other people. So absolutely, it's both an individual and a collective thing."*

According Terry McCabe, if young lawyers and law students are required to take individual responsibility over their own personal and professional lives, there first needs to be a legal culture and environment that supports, encourages and facilitates mental health programs:

> *"While I accept that there is a greater level of awareness, throughout our profession, of the enormous problems of mental health in law, I challenge my fellow managing principals directly across the legal profession to see what they are doing at an organisational level to address this issue. Work practices are still not significantly changing, so all of us need to challenge ourselves more. One of the things that I would really like to do for us is to have another look at our culture, and make sure that we can change it. I think it works on both levels; the level of the individual, and the level of the organisation. The individual won't act unless he or she feels a degree of empowerment, and ultimately that has to come from the organisation as well."*

This initiative then becomes the cornerstone for facilitating individual action. It helps young legal professionals feel empowered by those around them, especially those in power. It makes these individuals embrace the wellbeing practices that are available to them.

But isn't that a chicken and egg scenario? How can we get those in power to "up their game" so that we can, in turn, manage our own affairs?

That is a very tricky question, especially in regards to the quandaries of "Eleanor Robinson" and "Sunrise". The answer, I believe, lies in the responses of the interviewees listed in the previous chapters. According to Lucinda Clarke, development is resilience, and resilience is necessary to survive and prosper. Nick Edwards concurred when he remarked that, "No one is in a better place to look after yourself than you."

According to "Adelaide", a swift push may be necessary to jump-start the management of your health. "Robert James" and Sarah Beth agreed with their peers when they asserted that proactivity is the key to taking individual responsibility for your mental health, especially given that resources are available at your disposal.

By doing these things, you are essentially demanding the change you deem necessary in the legal profession. Truthfully, "Sunrise" would feel more empowered to request a sick day from her employer, and "Eleanor Robinson" would feel more confident in seeking assistance for any given scenario, if mental health were a priority at most, if not all, places of employment and universities.

It is important to understand that taking individual responsibility for your own actions is not simple to do. And no one should ever say that it is. But even trying to take charge of your health and wellbeing can make things easier for you. Moreover, with a little luck and sheer determination, it just might inspire the community to take a long-lasting stand on mental health issues.

TWD Wellbeing Wisdom

Not one interviewee (not even the most vocal critics) disputes the notion that each individual should take charge, to some extent, of his or her own existence. The significance of this burden is a matter for a later debate, among the interviewees; however what they can agree on is that you should make an effort to look after yourself to the best of your ability.

Jean-Paul Sartre once said that man is condemned to be free, for once he is thrown into the world, he is responsible for everything that he does. By accepting personal responsibility for yourself and your own situation, you consequently give yourself the freedom and authority to create your own life, in whatever way you want it.

Assuming individual responsibility for your mental health and wellbeing involves the following:

- Developing and/or practising resilience, especially in your work environment. Harnessing an internal drive to improve your own health and wellbeing, when applicable. Without this stimulation – progress will stagnate!
- Being fully aware of the existing resources available to you, regardless of how ineffectual or inapplicable you deem them to be, and being open to these options and ideas!
- Exploring and maintaining networks that will help you manage and manoeuvre your emotional and psychological states.
- Requesting and even pushing for greater assistance and support from your employer or institution, so that you can better help yourself and those around you.
- Relying only on yourself for validation, rather than external persons, circumstances or environmental factors.
- Forgiving yourself and others for any mistakes that may have been made, so that you can move forward in a healthy fashion.

Dr Fisher regarded these above suggestions as positive,

and noted that each individual needs to have in position a fundamental understanding of themselves and their place in the professional sphere.

> *"The first thing is to ask, 'What is my relationship with myself and how do I treat myself?'*
>
> *"Some people truly believe that they have the responsibility to look after everybody else, and that they come at the bottom of the pile. Rather, I would suggest that all relationships are fundamentally contractual in nature, including the relationship with yourself. It is certainly the case that the relationship with your employer is contractual. The question is, is the deal a good deal?*
>
> *"If you go into a law firm without doing your due diligence, it is no different from buying a secondhand car that has a lot of faults and finding that you crash and burn."*

This aptly concurs with what has been suggested in this chapter; ultimately, responsibility for your own health and wellbeing lies with you. Take charge of your own existence and be the best legal professional you can possibly be!

What works and what doesn't work when managing your health and wellbeing?

There are a multitude of issues, factors and causes that give rise to the prevalence and effects of depression, psychological distress and anxiety among members of the legal profession. While no single issue is solely responsible for ill health, any of them has the capacity to affect your wellbeing.

This chapter will discuss the primary issues that plague law students and young lawyers. It will also address how these issues can consequently interfere with the wellbeing of those individuals (i.e. law students and young lawyers). These issues will be addressed through a showcase of interview snippets from a plethora of legal professionals (from current law students to academics, judges and partners).

A large portion of the persons interviewed for this book are currently young lawyers. As a result, they are better able to engage with and/or relate to the plight of law students and young lawyers. It is also important to involve the perspectives of a broad spectrum of legal personalities because it is necessary to develop the most effective suggestions and tips.

This chapter will also highlight tips and suggestions that will help you thrive, rather than just survive, in a legal environment. These suggestions and tips will ultimately help you become the best legal professional that you can be.

Note: All of the comments, conversations, suggestions and references in this chapter were added by lawyers, created with lawyers, and developed for lawyers. As proclaimed at the outset of this book, there is no substitute for consultation with a medical professional. The thoughts expressed here by interviewees are anecdotal accounts of peer experience and support and should be taken as such.

What *does* work?

Despite my shortcomings and mistakes, there were a handful of things I was very good at when I approached my recovery. I tried hard to keep up activities that brought me joy, such as team sports and reading books, and I refused to shy away from seeking help or advice from other people. By and large, the perspectives and guidance of others was hugely helpful.

Lucinda Clarke:

> *"Finding a balance, and maintaining sufficient levels of self-respect and self-love are needed to push back when you're being pushed to the brink. Ask for help, and DO NOT BE AFRAID to say that you're having a hard time coping. I wish I'd realised this earlier and not three years in."*

While Lucinda and I have proved ourselves to be adept at maintaining our interest and passions, it is fair to say that not everyone can do this. For those legal professionals who find themselves lost for inspiration on this front, there are – thankfully – avenues available to you. There are a number of creative arts groups within the Australian legal community that have been established specifically for lawyers. The purpose of these groups is to encourage people to get involved with their communities. The goal is to not only ensure that lawyers establish and maintain a healthy work/life balance, but also to encourage legal professionals to maintain their passions.

Marie Jepson:

> *"I think if you can have a passion – that is incredibly important. There's a group of young lawyers in Melbourne who have set up a group called Bottle Snail Productions. This group does theatrical and comedic performances. Last year, it put on a play called the 'Twelve Angry Men'. All of the roles in this play consisted of barristers and lawyers. The role of the judge was actually performed by a judge, and his scenes occurred in a Supreme Court setting. In addition, 'Lawchestra' organises the 'Battle of the Bands' each year. This group also provides opportunities for creative people, within the law field, to explore more creative avenues, and to do them along with their practices. And, as a result, they are getting really positive responses."*

As with anything that you do, it is absolutely crucial that you have a proper routine in place. This necessarily involves not leaving important items to chance. You have to make time, rather than find time for the activities that matter to you.

> *"...The best long-term strategy for dealing with tasks is making sure that you've developed a good routine. Make sure that you factor in time not just for work, but booking things like exercising, reading a book, and/or catching up with friends. And one of the hardest things to do, when transitioning from law school to the legal profession, is to make time for your own*

needs. Why? Well, because things can get quite busy, which can cause individuals (especially law students and young lawyers) to neglect friends, and become isolated. Therefore, I would recommend that people organise breakfast or lunch solely for 'catch-ups'. Why? Well, because that is your time to do what makes you happy. And it's an opportunity to make sure that you have support networks, when you need them."

It is also important to remember that your educational and/ or vocational connections and communities can help you through some very dark periods. By virtue of being so heavily involved in on-campus life when I was a law student, and then having made strides with persons in the wider legal community, I was well placed to lean on the wisdom of friends and mentors at university.

Jade Tyrrell:

"What works well is the networks that are created in universities or in law societies, whether it be their respective social events or structured training and/or mentoring programs. I think that works incredibly well and also talking about these issues, as simple as it is…even if the university or the law society has a lecture about the importance of looking after health and wellbeing in the law. It doesn't have to be the elephant in the room. Every single time we talk about it, it breaks down the taboo surrounding depression and anxiety. So that's really important, and is an important tool that works well…putting it out there for discussion and for positive resolutions to come about as a direct result."

Another benefit that I enjoyed as a result of having been so immersed in the on-campus experience at UTS was that it gave me a greater appreciation for, and access to, the resources and information necessary for tackling depression in law. Admittedly, I did not utilise this unique position as well as perhaps I should or could have. But having it can be greatly beneficial.

According to Matthew Littlejohn, there is no substitute

for being well informed and prepared. He shares how mental health discussions helped him recognise the signs and symptoms of depression. As a result, he was better able to manage the onset of his condition.

> *"What works is recognising the warning signs, the early signs of depression or anxiety, and being self-aware enough to spot them, and do something about them. I hit my lowest point or worst point when I tried to push through, or ignore the symptoms. I honestly believed that I could go another week or a few more weeks, or until the end of exams."*

Aimee Riley elaborates on what Matthew Littlejohn espoused, when she states that the best way to protect legal professionals from experiencing psychological distress or developing depression and anxiety is to address the causes and symptoms associated with them early.

> *"What does work is admitting we have a problem. Not necessarily a problem, I think 'problems' may be an unfavourable label, but admitting that there's different factors that lend themselves to making a negative environment, and working on how we can address those issues."*

If you do, however, find yourself in a position in which your health issues have manifested to the point that you need to make significant changes in your life, it is important that you put your health and happiness first. I know this is easier said than done; especially when it comes to sharing information that makes you appear vulnerable, but it is necessary for recovery.

I felt that there was no other available option when I decided to open up to my previous employer about my health. If I didn't feel confident that I could survive full working days, what else could I do? What is paramount about this approach is that it places one's health and happiness at the top of the pecking order. It may seem like a last resort, and perhaps in some ways it is. But if your wellbeing is so damaged, then I say the best thing you can do for yourself, and those around you, is to be transparent.

What *doesn't* work?

Aimee Riley expanded on her previous comments by asserting that, if the legal profession is unable, as a whole, to acknowledge and support a person suffering from a mental illness or psychological distress, that person may be unable to achieve complete recovery.

> *"Being dismissive and saying, 'Oh, you'll be fine' or pretending it's not there doesn't work. In my opinion these issues really don't get the validation that is needed."*

We discussed in previous chapters the tendency of lawyers to be competitive and driven, sometimes overly so, which can result in health issues (physical and mental). According to James Tobin, that type of approach really does not solve the underlying problems commonly faced by legal professionals.

> *"What doesn't work is thinking that you can do everything, for everyone, all of the time. One of the hardest things to do – especially for young lawyers – is to say 'No' to a partner or senior associate, who comes, and throws some work at you, and says, 'Can you do this for me?' You have to be able to push back, and be realistic in your expectations of what you can and cannot do. There is no point of saying 'Yes' to everyone, and thereby putting yourself into a frenzy. Why? Well, because it will only escalate your stress. And it's the same for clients. If say a client says, 'Can I get this document by four o'clock tomorrow?' and you say, 'Yes' and you know that you have at least five other deadlines, it becomes unrealistic, and all you are doing is putting a huge amount of pressure on yourself. So you have to learn to be realistic about deadlines, and prepare to say 'No' to a client, if you don't have the capacity to do it at that time,*

> *or do it within a specified timeframe. Truth be told, that can be very hard for a young lawyer to do."*

It is important to surround yourself with people who care for you and/or who are able to help you when you need it, because it is paramount to your health and wellbeing. More specifically, dealing with issues alone, rarely, if ever, is a practical solution. "Elizabeth", a final year law student at a Sydney-based university who requested anonymity, discussed this.

> *"I find that I'm significantly more anxious when I'm on my own than when I am around a group of people, no matter what I'm doing."*

The same argument applies to reacting negatively to something you are experiencing. Being negative will only compound your problems.

"John":

> *"Remorseless self-deprecation, comparing one's own mental problems to those of others, marginalisation of one's own problems, doubling down, resentment because one feels sad typically occurs because one hasn't done enough work."*

"Rebecca", a law graduate from a top Australian law school, has not experienced the same health issues as others; however, she has witnessed the effects of mental illness in one of her closest friends, whom she feels worsened her condition by not acknowledging the signs of anxiety. This quote was made anonymous because "Rebecca" did not want the reader to extrapolate the identity of the friend she refers to.

> *"I look at someone I know, and I believe that she has issues with anxiety. She won't admit it because she's so headstrong. But she definitely has issues with anxiety and pressure, and the expectations she places on herself. And in that way she is quite reckless. She'll go out, and write herself off, and you can see that it takes toll on her."*

A problem can only be solved if solutions are put in place. If a law student or young lawyer is unable or unwilling to take steps towards recovery, he or she will never fully heal from his or her condition.

Nick Ferrari:

> *"It's when you recognise that you do have things like stress popping up, or that you're feeling unhappy with what you're doing, that you can do something about it. So when you recognise that you're starting to feel very, very stressed at work, or that you're starting to feel unhappy at your job – make a change. And that doesn't necessarily mean you have to leave the firm, or leave the profession altogether, it just means that if you're not happy where you are, look for something that will make you happy, and make the time to do it."*

Clary Castrission (a law graduate turned entrepreneur):

> *"...That was my problem – I didn't do anything to help myself. I didn't employ techniques. I just kept going, and yeah, it almost felt like I wasn't supposed to talk about what I was going through with anyone."*

In reflecting on my own health problems, I acknowledge that trivialising the issues I was facing, or employing a limited awareness in recognition of those issues, was a significant downfall. At times, I let my pride get in the way of better judgement. For example, it took me almost eight months to concede that anti-depressant medication was necessary to facilitate my recovery. Had I been willing to put in place the solutions that were required from an early stage, I could have fast-tracked my return from the brink. But by neglecting a remedy such as medication, I probably made things worse.

Don't make the same mistakes that I did...take on board as many solutions as you can and undertake the ones that are necessary for you and your situation.

TWD Wellbeing Wisdom

Professor Lesley Hitchens is the Dean of Law at the University of Technology, Sydney. This role allows her interaction with a great many students and academics, which gives rise to an educated opinion on this front.

> *"I don't think that it is because I think people are very different, and very richly diverse, in a sense. People have to find out what works for them, everyone's got to find their difference…for some it might be having a strong support of friends, or actually doing something physical, or even engaging in competitions and things like that. These things give you that kind of outlet and support. I think people have to find their own ways when it comes to that."*

As discussed in previous chapters, there is no right or wrong answer.

It is important to note that what works for you may not work for another person. But it is essential for your own health and wellbeing that you take action. In fact, to fail to do so, and/or to avoid action, is to allow issues of psychological distress, anxiety and depression to fester.

In light of this, here are lists of what you should and shouldn't do:

DO

- Settle into a healthy, consistent routine that works for you. This way, you will cease to neglect the things that matter most to you.
- Find and maintain a social network – this will be incredibly helpful for seeking support, and also supporting those around you.
- Be self-aware and knowledgeable about the signs and symptoms of depression in law – catching the warning signs early can be critical!
- Always put your health and happiness first, regardless of the

situation. Neglecting it will only spurn negativity and detrimental consequences for you and your work.

DON'T

- Be afraid to ask for help…it will always be there for those who seek it.
- Be dismissive of, ignore or minimise the suffering of yourself or others. Such health issues deserve validation and attention, no matter who is suffering.
- Try to do everything. Be aware of your capacities and limitations; rejecting help, or refusing to delegate, will only exacerbate your stresses.
- Bear the burden by yourself. Surround yourself with those whom you love – going it alone serves to increase anxiety and depression.
- Compare yourself to others; it is unhelpful because no two people are alike, and therefore your paths aren't comparable. Plus, you have no idea of the battles they may also be facing. Just be the best version of yourself that you can possibly be!

While these suggestions are useful points of guidance, ultimately one should consider their position from a more philosophical position. Dr Fisher identified a two-pronged approach to contemplating not only what works and doesn't work but also the value that you, the reader, place on your personal and professional life.

> *"I think that firstly you have to have a philosophy. What am I trying to do with my life and where does work fit into my life? I think that any mature human being has to ask that question. What are the pros and cons of doing what I'm doing, and what are the ramifications for the other parts of my life, particularly my non-work life?*
>
> *"I need to consider how much my work impacts upon my relationships with other people, my personal health and wellbeing, and how much time I have got to enjoy the things that are of interest to me outside of work. So the personal philosophy is one thing; secondly, it is important to know yourself.*
>
> *"If you know you're a highly anxious person and you are*

skewed to one end of the spectrum in this respect and are by nature vulnerable, the question is, 'Should I be in the law?'

"If I'm going to be in the law, what are the measures I can take to handle stress and to be resilient in the face of the stress that is known to be part and parcel of legal life?"

Giving proper consideration to your position will make it a lot easier for you to best identify what will work and not work in managing your own health and wellbeing in law.

It's so hard to find a job in law. What can I do?

In August 2013, *Lawyers Weekly* reported that the current period is the worst time in living history to be a law graduate.[34] In the post-GFC climate of the early 21st century, all young legal professionals are aware that the job market is tighter than it used to be, and finding full-time employment as a law graduate is tougher than perhaps it has ever been.

As any law student will tell you, summer clerkships with top commercial law firms and internships with leading public sector organisations are highly competitive. It can be demoralising and disenchanting to apply for jobs and then receive a negative response – or, in some cases, no response at all.

34 Leanne Mezrani, "It is the worst time in living history to be a law graduate" *Lawyers Weekly* (online) 27 August 2013 <http://www.lawyersweekly.com.au/news/14603-It-is-the-worst-time-in-living-history-to-be-a-law>

And as any newly admitted lawyer will tell you, graduate positions are also highly competitive, across the board. The aforementioned narrowing of the market is also exacerbated by a drastic increase in the number of law students, graduates, and, perhaps, the number of law schools. As a result, the profession is beholden to a market in which "even law graduates with excellent grades from top universities, who are also involved in numerous extracurricular activities, are rejected by law firms".[35]

So what can you do in the face of all of this stress and rejection?

This chapter provides guidance from lawyers with varying ranges of post-graduate experience. These lawyers offer excellent suggestions on how to best wade through the difficulties that law students and young legal professionals face when encountering the job market. And while it is true that no amount of positive reinforcement or reassurance will calm your anxiety and stress, it is essential that you try to keep certain things in mind. Why? Well, so that you can at least give yourself the best possible chance of managing your health and wellbeing during the most difficult times.

Manoeuvring and managing the job market

The search for jobs can be arduous and draining. You may sometimes feel that you will never get a job; that all of the good jobs have already been taken and ultimately your law degree may have been a colossal waste.

Sophie Waples describes the pressure and torment of going through the law job application process, and how it can

35 Ibid.

impact your psyche.

> *"Well, to put it bluntly, the job market is abysmal. If you can't get a job straight away, you have to do other things. You have to maybe do some more studying, or you have to remain active, you can't just let it defeat you, because things come up when you least expect it. But yeah, the job market has had a terrible impact on psychological wellbeing. I think I've always been on top of things. Luckily, I have been able to handle stress pretty well, but when I was finishing up uni [sic], and going through the clerkship process, and then, clerking at firms, it was probably one of the most stressful, if not the most stressful time of my life, and I don't think I've ever felt that before. You've just got to get out there, and meet as many people as possible, and try to remain positive."*

Many law students and young lawyers (including myself) can relate to the scenario above. It is incredibly difficult to anticipate, and consequently navigate this struggle, if and when it arises. Thankfully, however, there are a number of strategies that you can implement in order to combat any negativity that you suffer, as a result. According to "Eleanor Robinson", if you do find yourself in that position, there are certain things that you should bear in mind.

> *"If I was to give advice to someone, who has just come, and couldn't find a job, I'd say that, if you can, you should go travelling. I went through this, I fought, I can't even recall how long it was, but applying for jobs, and applying, and applying, and not getting anything. Accept that something will come in time. But there is something in acceptance, and in managing your own anxiety levels, and how you are feeling. Accept that it is hard, and accept that something is going to happen, but also accept that it is going to take a really long time, and during that long time, find other things that interest you – volunteer at a legal centre, volunteer in the community, etc. I think volunteer roles are easy to come by, and they keep you entertained, and engaged. If it's not the legal industry, what else are you*

> *interested in? And keep looking, but don't sit there every day – sitting at a computer applying for jobs day in and day out – you have to engage yourself in another way."*

This idea of keeping yourself busy while looking for jobs is paramount. It is crucial that you exercise other outlets that keep you stimulated, so that you are better able to maintain motivation for your main goal, which is to find employment.

The point about volunteering is important too, as while it may be a pit stop in finding a full-time position, and a way to fill hours during the day, there are professional benefits gleaned from those experiences. In fact, these experiences are invaluable, not to mention that you are making a tangible, positive difference in someone's life!

In late 2012, when I was sick and unemployed, I tried to break up the day into increments. In the morning, I would attempt to complete two to three job applications, and in the afternoon, I would go out to meet a friend, go for a walk, or workout at the gym – whatever took me away from the job hunt. It was so helpful to have this daily balance, because it distracted me from the frustration and the doubts surrounding my own self-worth (after submitting each and every job application), and it served to remind me that I had things in my life that weren't as aggravating; there were things that I still enjoyed, and could derive pleasure from.

Extrapolate your skills and interests

Another way of looking at this issue is that during this period of time, while you explore the job market, you are granted the freedom to find a role that truly suits your interests, skills and goals. It may even come in the form of something that you have not previously considered; but this is the time to properly identify what path you want to take in your career.

"Palm Tree":

> *"Just keep trying. It's easier said than done, but just look at the big picture. At the end of the day, you will get a job – it may not be your first choice of job to begin with, but you will eventually get the one you want. There's no point in over-stressing yourself about it. Plus, you're going to hate any job that you don't love. In other words, you're not going to do well under that sort of pressure. You might as well do a job that you love, and want to show up to every day. What's the point of putting yourself through five years of law school just to be miserable at your job?"*

Matthew Littlejohn reiterates the positive advice espoused by "Palm Tree", when he details the practical steps needed to identify the legal career that will best suit you.

> *"The first step is to really identify what your interests are; that takes some solid reflection and introspection as to what you really want versus what you think you might want. From there, you have to go beyond the university-issued careers guide and get onto company websites and see what they do. If it's a specific law firm, like a plaintiff law firm or a criminal career you want, find out if there is a committee of lawyers or people that work in that industry and see if you can join that. Speak to your university careers advisors. If you are a young lawyer I think that it does take a little bit of an initiative if there is a particular area that you want to get into; a career change doesn't just happen overnight. It never hurts to pick up a phone, and if there's one thing that I have learned and that crosses a whole a lot of other areas, it's that sometimes picking up the phone and just calling and asking saves a whole lot of time and can answer a lot of questions that you might otherwise spend a long time stressing over."*

In the struggle to churn out multiple job applications, and navigate your fluctuating stress and anxiety levels, in between those applications, this advice is extremely valuable (especially when reflecting on the types of applications you are submitting, and what kind of legal professional you ultimately want to be). Such rumination can afford you motivation and positive energy that you might, otherwise, not have during such a stressful period. Truthfully, it can be the difference between managing your wellbeing and becoming overwhelmed.

Control what you can

"Robert James" recommends that you realign your focus towards things that you actually have control over (namely the effort you personally put in), and let go of the things that you don't.

> *"The external factors you can't control; however, the internal factors you can. I think that law students should be proud of what they do, particularly when they can say that they've done their best. I think when law students can say that they have done their best, even if they didn't get any clerkship offers, or any graduate positions, or other seasonal internships, or any incredible volunteer positions in the Pacific Islands, I think they should still be proud of what they have done. Because, there is a lot of competition involved, and often that pride, and that sense of dignity really affects peoples' self-worth and self-value. I think that no matter what you do, if you do your best, you should be proud, and you will achieve your ultimate goals, and whether that takes you to different places, or whether you have to get to that goal through different means, well that's fine too.*
>
> *"It is also okay not to do your best sometimes. Well, you can't do your best all of the time, particularly in this economic climate of competition, so I think that law students, as well as being proud of their best, should also be proud when they can't do their best for some reason. This reason may actually be*

> *beyond their control (i.e. mental illness, stress, anxiety, and/or depression). So as you can see, it's really self-worth, self-dignity and pride."*

I'm a big fan of this suggestion. Being proud of your efforts and accomplishments may not, at face value, give rise to the job opportunity of your dreams. In addition, it is so easy to lose hope, to just give up, especially when it is hard to stay positive. But it is so important to stay consistent, when it comes to your health and wellbeing. It keeps you motivated to continue your search for meaningful employment.

Luke Furness:

> *"Persistence...I've had instances where I've needed to be really, really persistent. Getting a job as a paralegal, I think, I went through about 50 application processes. I got a job as a paralegal on my fifth application, and so, I always advise people that, if they want to break into the law – persistence is the key."*

If you can train yourself to stay positive, you will subsequently find that persistence is a skill that will come much easier. As a result, you will not only find that the job search is more productive, but you find out that your wellbeing is more consistent as well.

At the end of the day, however, there is no substitute for adequate preparation. Jade Tyrrell is a strong advocate for robust preparedness, and professes the following to law students and young lawyers when they approach the job market.

> *"I know for a fact that the market as it stands is one of the most difficult markets in the last few decades for law graduates. So that in itself puts a lot of pressure on students, as they graduate, lest they start to think about the options that are available to them, and because we've had clerkship opportunities in top-tier law firms in our faces for so long, I think we tend to forget about the alternative avenues and the other avenues that you can pursue. Those alternative avenues need to be made*

more readily available to students and to graduates especially, because it's almost as if you can't see the forest from the trees when you are focused so heavily on something that you should be doing as opposed to something that you could be doing or that perhaps you are better suited to be doing. I think the best thing somebody can do when they are a law student is to plan ahead really well. As soon as possible and even as early as your first year, it's best to start thinking about what tendencies you have, what interests you have, and how that can be made into a career because such a significant number of students try and fit into a mould where instead you can create your own opportunities. You can create your own parameters. I don't think law students and graduates (through no fault of their own) think about it in that way and I don't think that they really appreciate the value of other jobs that are available to them and jobs that may not earn them as much money, for example, but those that really are about helping people. They just need to realise or to be reminded of the vast array of possibilities."

While it is unlikely that you will be able to make an informed decision about your professional future at such an early stage, you should still give due consideration to your future, when presented with reasonable opportunities, so that you can draw on as much inspiration and information, as possible, when crunch time hits.

TWD Wellbeing Wisdom

ALSA:

> *"ALSA strongly believes in encouraging students to follow their passions and to pursue a career path which will provide them with as much gratification and satisfaction as possible – whether that be working in the private and commercial sector, to working in the public sector, to even pursuing a non-legal career. A law degree is incredibly diverse and can lead to a variety of equally fulfilling and satisfying career paths – it is important that law students take this into consideration when assessing their options in their penultimate and final years."*

Implementation of any or all of the following employment strategies will, I believe, put you on solid ground:

- It's never too early to think about your career. Soak up as much information as you can from the initial stages, and draw upon it, when the time calls for it.
- Find meaningful, productive distractions that will not only enhance your educational and professional skills, but also provide perspective in your day-to-day existence during the job hunt.
- Take the time to properly consider what vocational path you are best suited for, and dig deep for motivation to continue on your path for gainful employment.
- Focus your attention on the things you have control over, rather than the things that you don't. Worrying about externally influenced factors will not do you any favours.
- Practise resilience and persistence. Keep your strengths in your back pocket, because they will ease your emotional and psychological distress, while you search for a career.

Choosing the right job for me

Having fulfilling, revitalising work is considered a critically important component of recovery and wellbeing – even more so than cognitive behaviour therapy and medication.[36] Therefore, you must find work that satisfies you and makes you happy! Finding such work, however, can be harder than one might hope.

A common gripe for students and graduates is that law schools, careers sites, and fairs place too strong of an emphasis on advertising and/or advocating for corporate and commercial law careers, at the expense of other vocational paths that may better cater to the broader cohort of law students. This gripe is not necessarily unfounded – yet it is also not entirely a situation in which blame can be assigned to any party or even a group of parties. Law firms, generally speaking, have a greater fiscal

36 Cowan, n 11, 19.

capacity to promote and offer internships and employment opportunities, as well as the ability to sponsor law student society and/or on-campus events, when many not-for-profit government and other public interest organisations do not have the means to do the same. Consequently, the average law student feels that attaining a summer clerkship, securing graduate employment with a law firm and/or being chosen as a judge's tipstaff or associate, is the be all and end all.

This impression may be inaccurate, but it is persistent and widespread; and, as such, a significant number of law students and graduates find themselves opting for career paths that are inconsistent with their personalities, ambitions and/ or talents. As a result, these individuals put themselves at risk of not being able to attain the very job that they barely wanted in the first place. It is not a stretch to subsequently discern how issues of depression, psychological distress and anxiety can manifest within law students and young lawyers as they face their own existential crises in the aftermath of a demanding and competitive tertiary experience.

Of course, this does not have to be the case.

Professor McKeough:

> *"Be open-minded. There are so many jobs out there [in which you can] use your law degree. Even within the practice of law, there are so many niche things you can do."*

ALSA:

> *"ALSA believes that a career driven by passion will prove to be far more rewarding than a career driven by prestige or the promises of a high remuneration. In whatever career path law students ultimately choose, they must remember to find a balance between their work and their life commitments and to not forget the importance of protecting their health and wellbeing."*

There are a myriad of vocational paths that a graduate lawyer can go down, and a wide range of professional skills that can be utilised as a result of studying law. In fact, corporate and commercial law careers provide a multitude of fantastic opportunities for young lawyers. However, this is just one of many avenues that you should consider, especially if you are unsure about your career path. If you want to pursue a career in law – that is fantastic – go do it. But if you're interested in other things, explore those options as well! Law schools are well aware of the impression that the law field gives and they do aim to address it. However, law students and young lawyers also need to feel empowered and motivated to find legal careers that best suit them. The purpose of this chapter is to encourage you to not only have the courage, but also the will, to explore a vocational avenue that best suits your passions, gifts and values.

Learning how to pick the perfect career

Lucinda Clarke:

> *"No one ever found happiness doing what others thought they should do. Corporate law, for example, is definitely not for everyone. The idea that one specific type of job will suit all 350-odd people graduating from an annual university is ludicrous. A law degree should be recognised for what it used to be – an incredibly good grounding for an otherwise highly academic and industrious student (to open doors, but not necessarily just to law firms)."*

So don't go down a certain path if it's not for you.

But if you do want to pursue a particular career path in law, you need to be sure that you are on top of your personal, emotional and professional wellbeing, so that you are equipped to handle whatever circumstances are thrown your way. It is also important that you listen to law students and lawyers who have come before you (i.e. how their legal careers unfolded). "Robert James" discusses one of the most famous jurists in Australian history – The Hon. Michael Kirby AC CMG.

> *"Quite a few law students choose to follow a path that's imposed upon them by others, or even by themselves – by their own expectations about what they should do, but all paths in the law field contribute to personal and professional growth and society, so these individuals shouldn't necessarily feel that by not taking a job at a prestigious law firm, it is the end of their legal careers. For many, including Justice Kirby, who wasn't offered a graduate position at a big law firm, it opens other doors. I think that law students should choose a career path that suits their interests and their personalities, and not feel compelled to follow a path that has been set for them by others, or by their own expectations."*

You have to know where your skills and interests lie, and, then, know how best to utilise them.

Danny Gilbert:

> *"The leading corporate law firms attract a disproportionate number of the leading students. We should remember there are other options that provide perfectly rewarding career opportunities. There is this pressure that builds within the law schools which says that an indicator of success is a summer clerkship at a leading corporate law firm. I admire young students who are brave enough to say, 'Well, I don't need a summer clerkship, it's not for me and I really don't want to get onto this merry-go-round'."*

Competition among law students and young lawyers can manifest and lead individuals away from their personal values, and towards avenues that do not interest them as much, which in turn can cause a loss of self-esteem and wellbeing.[37]

Louisa Fitz-Gerald outlines a good strategy when thinking about what you want out of your career, and the best way to make it happen.

> *"...Try to think about core things that are important and not material things, necessarily. For example, is it important for you to be autonomous at work? Is it important for you to deal with businesses, or is it important to deal with people? Whose stories do you want to hear, and what do you want to help with? Do you actually like reading* The Australian Financial Review, *or did you just read it for your interviews, because you were worried that someone was going to ask you about an oil transaction? Once you answer these fundamental questions, you will be able to determine what you actually like. And, as a result, you will have a better picture of your career path, which is, 'I always wanted to be a lawyer, and now I'm here, so I can't give that up. Do you know how many people wanted to be here?' When you think about what you want to achieve, you can say, 'My ultimate goal is to have a satisfying career, where I'm autonomous, where I help people, where I do this, etc.' But I think we need to back away from material goals and striving for things without thinking about why we are striving for them."*

Anthony Lieu co-founded (and is the Managing Director of) the website, *Beyond Law*, a job website for law students, graduates and young lawyers. It offers a wealth of opportunities, not only in the commercial law field, but also in other fields, such as non-profit organisations and international judiciaries. The purpose of *Beyond Law* is to change the dialogue of legal professionals – to show law students and young lawyers

37 Paula Baron and Judith Allen, "Buttercup goes to law school: Student wellbeing in stressed law schools" (2004) 29 (6) *Alternative Law Journal* 285.

what they can do with a law degree. Anthony discusses the importance of being aware of the different career avenues, and taking the time to investigate the various ways that your career can unfold.

> *"The reality is, there are a lot of opportunities out there that students may know little about, and, then, from that, there's a lot of stress, and added stress that they need to only follow this one path, which can affect their wellbeing and/or how they perform in law school, or in their personal lives. But if they're aware of what else is out there, it relieves their stress, opens more doors, and makes them think about what else is out there.*
>
> *"Obviously it's the passion that you feel in what you do, and whether you want to change the world, or whether you want to work in a field that you're most interested or passionate about. In other words, it drives what you do. And, as a result, you put more love into what you do. In the end it just makes you a better person, a happier person. So rather than taking the mainstream path, ask yourself, 'What avenues can I take, in regards to my career?' It just makes more sense to do something that you're more passionate about. In fact, the reason you entered law school was to be able to do what you wanted to do."*

According to Clary Castrission, there are numerous career avenues that you can take as a result of studying law. Awareness of the options available to you, rather than feeling trapped by, supposedly, limited paths, can be very reassuring and comforting when considering how to begin your legal career.

> *"Law is a great profession; there are hundreds of different ways that you can practise. But I think that, depending on who you are, there are certain pull factors that pull you into certain paths that may not necessarily be the one that's most natural to you. I encourage you to go and have a look at the amount of people that choose advanced corporate law as an elective compared to those who choose something like international law, or sports law, or something that they've got inherent passions in, but then*

go and have a look at students who actually follow careers in sports law or international law. It becomes more a huge swing."

Once you are able to identify a job that you want, it is then important to deduce whether or not you will find it intellectually and emotionally stimulating. Having this insight will provide you with the motivation and drive needed for your position, as opposed to a role that you do not feel strongly about.

Senthorun Raj:

"I feel like in a lot of jobs, and this is not just specifically in corporate law, some people just feel really alienated from their work, it's deadening, it's boring, it's repetitive, it's overwhelming because they have to do a lot of it. I'm sure there are people out there who love corporate law, who find it energising, who find it interesting, who find it stimulating, and so it's not a question necessarily of the work, but more about the system and the processes, and so it's about whether people can feel supported to do what they do and make a contribution and feel stimulated by it. I think that's the question."

But even if you are unable to get it right the first time, Professor Lesley Hitchens reminds you that you live in a fortunate time, in which you are not expected to be stuck with a particular job for your entire career. You have the freedom to move around in order to find professional satisfaction and fulfilment.

"I think one of the advantages of graduates today, even though in some ways it seems tougher, is that nobody expects you to stay in a job long-term, and in my mind, from someone who's much older, and who went through a different experience, that seems to be quite a tough environment, but in a way, I think it allows people to feel that they're 'free' enough to move around, and not have the same loyalties they once had toward their job and employer.

"So if something isn't working for them, they can move off and try other things. So they can benefit from the experiences

they have, but still feel free enough to move around."

This is an important thing to remember. In fact, I feel strongly that, unless you feel completely certain that your decision to follow a particular career path is right, you should find a role that makes you happy, rather than falling into a role and hoping that you grow to like it. If you find a job that is fulfilling and enjoyable, at least for now, things will fall into place from there.

There is significant merit to the idea that you will perform better in a job that best suits your passions, gifts, and values, as opposed to a different line of work.

Nick Edwards:

> *"If law students and young lawyers follow a career path that suits them, I think they'll have a more fulfilling legal career. I think it also means that people will be better suited to the tasks at hand. In other words, they will have a more realistic expectation of what they will be doing and achieving, and they will be happier people who are fitted for their jobs. I think the problem with law is that there is a disparity between law student expectations and law firm expectations."*

Maxine Evers notes that if the level of autonomy and freedom that you experience in your job is more in line with your vocational ambitions, you will perform better.

> *"I think there's a good chance that you will be happier and more successful because you will be doing something that you, perhaps, are more passionate about. And, as a result, you may end up with more power over or more choice."*

"Palm Tree":

> *"I think that you're just gonna [sic] hate a job that you don't love. There's no point in working for a big law firm if you hate*

> *that kind of law. You're not gonna [sic] do well under that sort of pressure. You might as well do a job that you love, and want to show up for every day. What's the point of putting yourself through five years of law school just to be miserable in your job?"*

And in case you're in need of even more convincing, let's break this down into simpler terms – you are more likely to appreciate, understand, and therefore, put more effort into a job that you feel passionate about, enjoy, and are motivated to do. There is no disputing this idea; our motivation levels significantly increase when we feel emotionally attached to a given task.

TWD Wellbeing Wisdom

When selecting a job or career path, remember the following things:

- Don't follow a particular career path just because you feel like you should be doing it. Rather, only choose a career path if it is what you actually want!
- Have the courage to follow a career path that best suits your passions, gifts and values.
- Take time to decide what is really important to you professionally, so you can accurately identify the best career avenue for you.
- Familiarise yourself with the myriad opportunities available and once you earn a law degree – give adequate consideration to all opportunities.
- Don't place too much emphasis on any particular role, especially if you do not feel motivated by it. Remember, you have the flexibility to adapt to and evolve in your legal career!
- And, lastly, don't ever lose faith in your abilities. You are a valuable employee!

Dr Fisher regarded these suggestions as, "motherhood statements, which I fully endorse", and approved them. Additionally, he proffered sage wisdom in deducing the right career path for each individual, which aptly complement the suggestions listed above.

> *"One very important thing is the need for law students and young lawyers to understand that there is more than one choice of career path once you have successfully completed a law degree.*
>
> *"Every job comes as a package. It is just sensible to analyse what are the pros and cons of different packages. It may even be that you see your law degree as a sort of primary qualification that shows that you can think logically and then you go into a different profession, occupation or business.*

"Getting a grasp of the way in which a particular job operates on a day-by-day basis and how it unfolds over time is your responsibility before you leap into the breach.

"A mature, civilised human being should try to live as well balanced a life as they can and have non-work related sources of fulfilment and happiness.

"It makes increasingly good sense to try to diversify your source of income as soon as you can so that you are not so reliant upon the legal job."

How can I manage an often onerous workload in law?

Patrick Schiltz wrote that every hour that lawyers and law students spend working and studying is an hour that they do not spend doing things that give their lives joy and meaning. According to Schiltz, there is no mystery about why lawyers are so unhappy. They simply work too much.[38]

Of course, this is applicable to any person working in any profession but I have found that, in my experience, it has an unusual effect upon law students and young lawyers. One of the more peculiar circumstances that I have witnessed is the fact that young legal professionals do not seem to recognise that the sheer volume of work that they do is greater than people in most, if not all, other professions. I have actually

38 Schiltz, n 31, 895.

lost count of the number of times that a graduate lawyer friend has proclaimed excitement, or more accurately, relief, at being able to leave the office at 8pm or 9pm, rather than having to stay late into the night.

It baffles me how young lawyers cannot fully comprehend and accept the ramifications and consequences. How can we, as young legal professionals, be so detached from what other people consider to be a normal working day? It is no wonder that the rates of depression are so high in the legal profession.

Lawyers Weekly reported in late 2014 that, "…lawyers are churning out work at an unhealthy rate, which is impacting their job performances and their mental health".[39] It is time that this trend was reversed.

This chapter evaluates the volume of work that is required, not just in legal practice, once you are a lawyer, but also in the number of hours of study often required for success in law school. (Note: Success means different things to different legal professionals, thus some will dedicate an even greater number of hours to the pursuit of good grades and job opportunities.)

It is important to have an arsenal of study strategies to adequately complete the tremendous amount of work often required. This chapter delves into those strategies in an effort to help you better manage whatever tasks may be at hand.

Prioritise other things in your life

Studying and working long hours can be draining, both physically and emotionally. And this is just an immediate outcome – in the larger sense, these activities can have

39 Mezrani, n 33.

a significant impact on your daily health and wellbeing, particularly your levels of stress and anxiety. Louisa Fitz-Gerald emphasises how this can materialise.

> *"I think whenever I have conceptualised my own mental health, the image that I use is a table that has several legs, like lots and lots of legs. My mental health is the tabletop, and each one of the legs is something that holds it up. Friends are one, sport is one, work is one, and family is one...it goes on and on. I think that what those excessive hours do is prevent you from having other legs. You can't see your friends, you can't do your sport, you can't have your interests, you can't go dancing, and you can't do whatever it is that interests you.*
>
> *"I think it makes you so much more susceptible to the ups and downs at work. Something bad happens at work, and if that's your only leg, it will crumble a little bit, and your mental health will really start to tip. So that's a real problem, I think not letting people have outlets, and other parts of their lives is really, really damaging. I also think that young people can change it themselves. I mean, they just don't have to be there, and a much quicker fix is for a law student or a lawyer to just study or work where they want to, rather than where they feel they need to."*

I love Louisa's analogy of the table with multiple legs, and not just because it directly correlates to my personal analogy of standing on a glass floor that gets thinner or thicker depending on what is happening in my life at that particular time. Discussing your support systems in the manner that Louisa does drives home the importance of having things in your life that will not only give you balance, but also revitalise you and your career (legal or non-legal) in so many wonderful ways.

This point about choosing your own path is something that Luke Furness also picked up on. It is an important argument, in terms of how you decide to study law, and what direction you want your legal career to take.

"I've had senior partners in my firm say everything from, 'This is a 24/7 business, and you just have to get used to it' to senior partners saying, 'This is a marathon, so don't run out too early, go home, develop hobbies, and/or everything in between'. I think you'll find university lecturers who say the same thing – that some are very pro-competition, while others sit back, relax and have fun. So I think it definitely varies in terms of the people. I do wonder, sometimes, whether clients believe that everything is super urgent. I think that overall, as a profession, we do a pretty poor job of setting our own standards (of what we will and won't accept), and I think there are pockets, both in law school and in the firms, in which people strike back with more of a work/life balance."

Practise efficiency and discipline

I always find it incredibly helpful to write a list of things to be completed. While it may consume some time in those initial stages, I am always much better off for having taken those few minutes to prioritise and coordinate my plan of attack.

This can become incredibly important when faced with cultural idiosyncrasies in law. According to Sophie Waples, the somewhat ridiculous culture surrounding work hours can appear, to outsiders, as a kind of competition between lawyers.

"I think there is a real perception – once you get into the workforce – that if you're not doing the long hours, then you're not working hard enough. If you say to other lawyers that you got out at 5pm, everyone is shocked, and says, 'Oh, it must be quiet at work,' and it's almost like a negative response, as opposed to saying, 'Good for you,' people think that there is a correlation between the hours you work, and your success, or

importance, or achievements, which is a real pity, because you should be able to have your own life outside of work, and be equally successful, and feel like, if you do finish your work on time, you're not letting anyone down. If you've done your work – you should get out."

How do you respond to this? By being as efficient and productive as you possibly can. Be in the office, then get out, and enjoy what's left of your day, because you will be more refreshed, and therefore more effective when you return to work the next day. More specifically, you will dispel, for yourself and others, why there is an inherent need to stay late. Of course, staying late is sometimes necessary and a required duty to your employer; it is also important to fight whatever competitive or perfectionist traits you may have. In other words, do what is best for you!

Lucinda Clarke believes that making sure your work is efficient is not as difficult as it may sound.

"I'd say learning efficiency is an incredibly important tool. Don't sit around all day on Facebook and then find you have to stay late at 6pm. Do whatever you can, do it as best you can and as quickly as you can, then get the hell out of there at 6pm, whenever possible, and go live your life."

Exercise transparency and open communication

"Mary", a solicitor with a mid-tier Australian commercial law firm who asked not to be named, offers an additional approach, which is to communicate effectively with your superiors and colleagues, so as to give yourself a good chance of being able to achieve efficiency.

"There's definitely an expectation that you'll work long hours.

> *There's also, in some cases, an expectation that you won't question it. I've been lucky enough where I'm working, that there is a focus on having a work/life balance and having people that you can go to if you feel like you're burning out, which is really positive. When I started working, I would just stay late until things were done, I wouldn't necessarily ask questions. I felt like I didn't want to show that I couldn't do something or that I couldn't figure it out for myself, when really, looking back now, if I had asked questions, I could have fast-tracked a lot of things. So I think it's a case of asking questions of your superiors when you need to. In terms of taking care of yourself and your health, make sure to make time to see friends and family and spend time doing the things you like doing."*

Having that dialogue with people around can reap rewards that you may not have previously considered. Perhaps there is someone in the office to whom you can outsource the work, or maybe your superior can dedicate some time from his or her schedule to assist you? Is it possible that you and your study partner can combine forces on a task to fast-track completion of an assignment? Don't be afraid to have that conversation!

Set achievable goals

Another way to be efficient is to set yourself reasonable, achievable goals when you have what would, otherwise, be perceived as a mammoth task in front of you. Goal setting helps clarify exactly what is required and the timeframe in which you can accomplish a certain task.

Professor Lesley Hitchens advises law students and young lawyers to approach tasks in increments to make them less overwhelming.

> *"If you look at the Great Wall of China or Hadrian's Wall, it looks overwhelming but in the end it was built stone by stone. So if I'm trying to do something, it's about breaking it down – thinking what I have to do here – thinking this gets me to the first step, then this gets me to the next step, so I think it's just being very practical, and taking it in very small steps, whether it's around a subject, whether it's around an assignment, whether it's around thinking about all of the things that I need to acquire, in order to be a lawyer – all of the skills and understanding.*
>
> *It is day-by-day-by-day, and I think the other thing is students should to try as much as they can, and work with what is in the present, not always planning everything out for the future. In other words, not trying to think everything is about how it will look on my CV, but how it will work for me at that moment. Can I manage this, and do I want to do, and still build from there?"*

Professor Hitchens makes a fantastic point. In fact, it is one that I have practised myself. In the final semester of my law degree, I found it immeasurably difficult to focus on completing my law readings each week, as I was coming to terms with my depression. But by breaking down my readings into smaller segments I was able to digest the information. Every time I finished a page, or even a paragraph, I took a mental and physical break. I closed the book, got a glass of water, or did a lap of the house.

This, together with the unconditional support I received from my girlfriend at the time (who also doubled as a study partner), meant I was able to get through that final semester unscathed.

Choose the right cultural fit for you

James Tobin analysed how different workplaces instil their own cultural practices upon employees.

> *"[Long hours] can have a huge impact, as a general rule. I'd say that the volume of work in law is great, but at the same time it can be as much or as little as you want it to be. It depends on where you want to be, and what you want to be doing. It's fair to say that sometimes you're expected to work 12–14 hours a day and it's not unexpected for you to come in and work on the weekends, whereas in other places, you can probably get away with working from 8am–6pm most days, and not come in on the weekends. So it's where you pitch yourself in the market, as to what you want to be doing, whether you want to be a barrister, or partner, or high-flying person. But if you are quite comfortable just earning a decent lifestyle, and doing some good work, you can manage that. So you need to understand and pitch yourself as to which lifestyle or what balance you want to have in your work/life relationship."*

As such, it is important for you to choose a workplace (whether you are a graduate lawyer looking for full-time employment or a student looking for a paralegal position) that best suits the number of hours you feel comfortable working.

Note: This does not equate to a black and white scenario of choosing between the public or private sectors – commercial law firms have a reputation of demanding long hours from their employees. However, I have friends in those firms who work comfortable hours, and I have friends who work for legal aid services who are stuck at their desks until late at night and sometimes on weekends.

It is important for you to take the time to glean what you can about a workplace's culture, so that you can determine if it fits with your personality/lifestyle, and if it is really what you want from a legal career. Depending on your workplace, it may also be possible to insert activities into your life at the office in order to better manage the long hours and also achieve a balance.

Kate Taylor has noticed this at her firm as an indicator for successful time management.

> *"The people that I have spoken to, while I've been at work, who seem to be dealing with the hours the best, are the ones that take advantage of the free gym membership or join social clubs within work to try and balance out the work/life divide. I know it sounds kind of ridiculous when the workplace encapsulates things in your life. But if you're going to be there 15 hours a day, you might as well try and enjoy those things as well."*

Set time limits – be strategic and avoid perfectionism

Admittedly, it is not always possible to be efficient and productive. "Elizabeth" discusses how these episodes have affected her, and how best to react to them.

> *"It definitely wears you down. Sometimes, I really find it hard to keep up with everything, and it has gotten to the point where I have to accept that I can't work on particular weekends, even though it is my only time to work, because I am so run down, and if I try and do more study, then I am just not going to be able to cope. So I have had to put in specific barriers, and tell myself 'yes', you are not going to work this weekend, and you probably won't do that assignment you wanted to do, but the balance is to lose a few marks, or potentially not be able to submit the next one, because I am exhausted.*
>
> *"I think in the workplace, it is a little bit different, because you have someone else breathing down your neck, it is really hard to say no. That is something I am really concerned about because I know that if they say 'we need you here can you come in?' I will respond with 'yes, what time do you need me here?'. I think at a junior level at least saying 'no' is very difficult."*

In practising efficiency, however, it is possible to be strategic, by way of allowing yourself a certain time frame in which you complete a task, and also avoiding the tendency to second-guess your work and return to it.

This is not to say that you should be complacent about mediocrity. But continuing to work on a task that you have already completed, or spending too much time on it, cannot be beneficial either. Setting a time limit and sticking to it can provide you with fresh motivation to not only finish a given assignment, but do it to a level that you can be proud of. "Monty" discussed how he was able to manage the more onerous period of his law degree, and how he has adapted his strategic processes to acclimatise to life in the workforce.

> *"I think that for me, it was just a matter of playing the game. By the end of your law degree, you know what the markers want. Usually you can get away with not doing much in class and then come exam time you cram. You play the exam game well and get the marks you need, and that is it. In practice, I think the pressure on time spent is a bigger concern and I think I've come to realise that law is a service-providing industry – you are at the beck and call of a client; if your client is operating at a different time zone, you still have to be there. Having work email on your phone is pretty demanding – you can have that 24/7 and some partners expect you to be there within the hour of an email coming through, others are more relaxed. Legal practice is much more of a time demand than in uni for sure."*

Although "Monty" did not note how best to strategically manage his workload and himself in the workforce, as compared to his experience in law school, it is possible to extrapolate that the same principles apply: understand and appreciate what is expected of you in order to perform at a level that satisfies your teachers, superiors and clients, and figure out how to best to make it work in the context of looking after your own mental health and wellbeing.

This strategy can manifest in other ways. Professor Hitchens addressed whether or not law students can or should take on commitments in addition to their already demanding study schedule.

> *"Law is a demanding course, and nobody can say otherwise because of the nature of the vast amounts of written work, but at the same time, it's not designed to be overwhelming. People need to work out efficient ways to study and take breaks. The classroom is supposed to take a certain amount of time and preparation, and assignments are going to take up a certain amount of time. Often what takes up a lot of time, as well, is all of the other activities that students participate in, and I think that's great because there's a lot of community in that, a lot of opportunities for student to interact, and enjoy each other's company, through that shared enterprise.*
>
> *"Students have very busy lives, because they take on a lot of those things. I do think, and it's easy to say when you're a lot older, not everything has to be accomplished at once, and I think often students think that everything has to be accomplished at once. There will be time to do other things, and I do think that's quite important. Thinking about how much time is given to a whole range of activities, and I think that's all good, but just bearing in mind how much people are taking on, and whether some things are being sacrificed. It's better to do a whole lot of things well, than a whole lot of things not terribly well, and to get completely exhausted trying to manage all of those things."*

This does not mean that law students, or young lawyers for that matter, should not involve themselves in extracurricular activities. Such a proposition would be contradictory to what I advise in other chapters (which suggest that you have a healthy work/life balance). But you should be wary of the capacity (as we, legal professionals, tend to do) to take on way too much, to try to achieve more than is possible, and ultimately end up burning out (as I did). Therefore, you should be strategic when selecting the commitments you undertake – outside of classes and/or work, so that your work/life balance doesn't become a crowded schedule that is suddenly unmanageable.

TWD Wellbeing Wisdom

Schiltz commented that the biggest complaint among legal professionals was increasingly long workdays in conjunction with decreasing time for personal and family life.[40] A culture in which a lawyer lives to work – instead of working to live – is one that may subsequently be fraught with psychological distress. More specifically, the result of such hours may result in a scenario in which a legal professional has to sacrifice, rather than dedicate, his or her life to the profession.[41]

Thankfully, there are ways to effectively manage long hours associated with studying and practising law. These strategies include:

- Making an effort to have many "strings in your bow".
- Refraining from overloading yourself to the point that there are too many strings, and you cannot effectively find a healthy work/life balance.
- Staying above the cultural fray that may encourage putting in unnecessarily long hours. Practise reasonable and successful efficiency at work.
- Figuring out how you can strategically manoeuvre your way through the work day, so as to negate the potential for working long hours.
- Breaking down the barriers of a given task, and segmenting them into smaller, more achievable tasks, so as to avoid a sense of being overwhelmed.
- Following educational and vocational paths that allow you to study and work in an environment that best suits your passions, gifts and values.
- And ALWAYS taking the time to recover and recuperate, whenever you feel affected by the amount of work you have to complete. As a result, you will be healthier and happier that ever before!

40 Schiltz, n 31, 880.

41 Ibid.

How can I unwind when I'm stressed at my desk?

Sometimes, it doesn't matter how seemingly balanced and holistic your life is: stress can still hit you at any time. It's not a reflection on how organised you are, it is just that sometimes life throws a curveball that increases your anxiety levels.

It can happen when a tight deadline pushes you to your limit, or when you're given a task that dramatically increases your workload. It can also happen when you are pressured to complete assignments (especially, when you are not used to the pressure), when you have an assessment or exam coming up, and/or when you are trying to understand a topic, but simply can't wrap your head around it.

According to Dr Fisher, it is crucial that you implement the correct approach from the start. This necessarily involves outlining the most appropriate routine for you to undertake your work or study, and adhering to it.

> *"The deal you do on day one at the office is often the best deal you do. For example, I will take an hour off at lunchtime... that's my time off, I'm not here. I might be here, but I will be unavailable and I'm very strict about that. That's the deal that I do with myself and with my patients and referrers. I'm not available in that time and I get out and often go for a walk or have lunch or whatever else out of this office.*
>
> *"However, I am my own employee; the extent to which you can do things within a law firm is not necessarily the same thing. So the question is how you try to clarify what are the employer's expectations of you and your expectations of them.*
>
> *"You try to establish good habits from the beginning.*
>
> *"It is often helpful to 'compartmentalise' and draw lines under certain issues to make certain you have time for yourself. It is up to you to enforce those boundaries and avoid constantly giving in to people asking, 'Oh, but can't you just do this for me?'*
>
> *"There are good ways of responding to this. These include saying, 'I would love to do that for you, but if I do that, I will not be able to complete other tasks you have given me. I can see Joe Bloggs over there without enough to do, I'm sure he can help you out.'*
>
> *"Indeed, if you say that you have to have a break and that you will get on with the job with a much fresher frame of mind once you have had your lunch, then this will generally be appreciated by your managers. Most mature employers will see this as assertive self-caring behaviour. They will note that you are able to look after yourself, that you are reliable, and that you are not going to be lost to the firm because you don't look after yourself properly."*

We all get stressed! There's no shame in it, and sometimes there's not a lot we can do about it. Thankfully, there are things that you can do to alleviate stress whenever it hits you, and safeguard against the onset of anxiety that may arise as a result of being tied to your desk.

Some of the suggestions in this chapter may seem simplistic.

But that's what makes them so useful. In fact, these steps can relieve the pressure, with very little effort. Contrary to popular belief, stress management techniques do not have to be overly complicated. In fact, the only barrier you may face, while undertaking these steps, is a lack of desire to actually get out of your chair and away from your desk.

Stepping outside the office

"Peter":

> *"I have been going out at lunch time lately. There is a bit of a culture around staying at your desk the whole time, and staying at your desk at lunchtime; some people do it because they want to leave early. They eat their lunch at their desks because then they can leave early, while others do it because they want to complete their billable hours and leave. If you are doing that, well that's probably fine, because you are still not working too much, and you are leaving earlier, but I think it is a good idea just to say, 'Okay it's lunch time, I'm just going to go and walk down the street, sit somewhere, have a sandwich or whatever, come back, and just take another break.'*
>
> *"Try and take a break every couple of hours or whenever you get up from the desk, and go drink too much coffee just because it is something to do. But I think all that is necessary, and people forget about it because they feel pressured, and they feel anxious, and there will be people saying, 'Where's this, where's that, and whatever?' But you know five minutes, 10 minutes, or 15 minutes, or even a half-hour...things aren't going to fall apart if you just take a breather for that short period of time."*

It can be very tempting to skip your lunch break when you are a graduate lawyer, student paralegal, or summer clerk who is working hard to impress superiors. Powering through the day, sans lunch break, may seem, at first instance, to be a strategic move to appear as productive as possible.

I have also been guilty of this. But the most striking thing about skipping the lunch break, compared to taking a 30- to 60-minute break, is that I feel less stable and energised, compared to when I make the effort to step out of the office. I have found that my productivity and attention to detail is much greater when I have had that distance from my desk. As "Peter" asserts above, things won't fall apart if you step out of the office for a short period of time.

Let's not forget that workplace laws require employees to take at least a half-hour break when working more than six hours a day. So make sure that you take your breaks because they help you re-focus and clear your mind. They also help reduce stress and boost energy, so that you are productive and energised at work.

"Katherine", for one, has discovered that allowing herself a quick break is not going to be the end of the world and, when compared to how she used to practise her daily routine, she is much better equipped to get headspace and reinvigorate herself.

> *"I think sometimes stepping away, even if it's just for five or 10 minutes and getting some perspective on what you're doing is really crucial. It's not something I'm good at doing when I'm in a high-pressure situation, but I need to remember to use these tools. When you're wound up and in a stressful situation you think that every single second should be spent on that task that you're doing, so sometimes you step away and realise that five minutes away from your desk will give you some perspective."*

Listening to music

Luke Furness:

> *"I often sing when I'm nervous – it takes the pressure off, believe it or not. I sing when I'm happy, but I sing when I'm nervous, as well, and I often listen to music. You can shut the door when everything is going a bit pear-shaped, and you just want to relax. Music isn't everyone's thing, but that is definitely the strategy that I use."*

What I love most about Luke's "music-for-relaxation" strategy is that it is his own personal approach to stress-relief. Over the years, I have learned that the things closest to your heart are the same things that can ultimately calm you down when you start spiralling out of control.

Ever since I was in high school, I found that music minus the lyrics was the best approach for me, because lyrics would distract me from the task at hand. Classical compositions became my tunes of choice, as they are calming and serene, and I have never looked back!

I often employ my iPod whenever the stress builds up and being at the desk is too monotonous or mundane. Further, having such background music can give you a kick-start on your motivation levels, thus making you more productive.

Mindfulness and meditation

"Robert James":

> *"I use awareness and meditation techniques; these were taught to me by a few counsellors that I saw in the past. In terms of the awareness techniques, it basically revolves around reconnecting with your surroundings, and becoming aware of the minute things around you, which really centres your focus. In terms of*

> *meditation techniques, they often involve breathing, and I like to use meditation techniques, as well, because they focus me, and focus my thinking, as well as making me feel very relaxed."*

According to Joel Orenstein, in the past decade, legal practitioners have increasingly turned to meditation to not only combat stress and depression, but also to enhance general health and wellbeing. It is a useful practice for lawyers to consider, because meditation provides an avenue through which you can be "aware of your thoughts and emotions instead of being thrown by them. It also a space, in which you can just let go".[42]

"Adelaide" utilises similar stress-management techniques to calm herself.

> *"Then and there, I'd get up, and go for a walk, I breathe very deeply – I do deep breathing exercises. I share with someone… I'd walk into my neighbour's office across the hall, or to the senior associate, who supervises me, and I'll 'offload'. We do a lot of 'offloading' in our team, even just for little pressure valves, even if it's not big stress, and I think, maybe, that's how we cope with stresses at a broad level.*
>
> *"You are releasing your pressure valves multiple times a day, by just little comments, so we don't let that stress accumulate… so, that you end up in tears, because it's not hard to do. Stress in my experience is kinda [sic] like bits and bits and bits, and you can handle a couple, but it's when you have 40,000 tiny bits of stress, which can really can knock you down. And, it's like sleep, you know, you can do one night on four hours sleep…that's fine, you can function the next day, and you can do another night, but can you do 20 nights? No, it's not sustainable, and so, in our team, we 'offload' regularly, and in a way that is not always deep. It's just about getting some pressure off, cracking a joke and saying, 'Did you hear what he just said to me?' or 'That client drives me nuts', or something like that. And, it's possible*

42 Orenstein, n 7.

to, I think, release the stress in a positive way.

"So those are examples of what I do when I'm feeling more anxious than just the everyday stresses. I have a lot of good friends at work, and there have been times when I've gone in and had a crying friend at work, probably about three times, and what I find interesting is that often the 'upset' is not always work-related…it's life-related, and you just work a high pressure job, so that high pressure gets everything else going."

When I worked in the public sector, my employer offered weekly meditation and relaxation classes, which any staff member could attend during office hours. I have never been terrific at this kind of discipline, for the reason that I find it very difficult to switch off and stop thinking about a million different things at once. But when you are finally able to achieve that state whereby you can be single-minded and dedicate your focus to your surroundings and your breathing, a wonderful sensation overwhelms you: it is the feeling that you are in complete control of your body and emotions.

If you can achieve this, you will find that your level of authority over stress and anxiety becomes much greater, and therefore managing those feelings is easier than ever before.

Social endeavours

Another outlet that people often use to relieve stress during a hard day's work is to have a drink or two – at lunchtime. On occasion, this may be helpful, in that it removes you from your office environment, and places you in a more socially relaxed setting.

Terry McCabe:

"…The other thing, which I do personally, which I don't recommend to anyone, and I have come in and out of this at

> *various times, is, if stress for me, is really bad (and I don't think I'm alone in this) when I go to lunch with a client, I find that the amount of vino that I consume might increase if I'm feeling stressed. And, while illegitimate, I think it is a commonly used aid that helps people get through a situation that is causing them a lot of stress."*

Personally, I've never been one for a tipple in the middle of the day – as I would likely fall asleep! But if it does help you disentangle yourself from the problems you are facing (and it is okay with your boss!), then I'd say that there isn't much harm in the occasional glass – as long as it is done in moderation and not too frequently. We will examine the place of alcohol in the lives of law students and young lawyers in a later chapter.

Preparedness and organisation

It is always recommended that you use a healthy outlet to relieve your stress. If you start to feel stressed, take a few minutes to adequately plan your approach to the tasks in front of you. Developing a solid plan has always helped me see the bigger picture. It is also advised to break down larger, more complex workloads into more manageable ones. This approach has the effect of making the work seem less overwhelming.

Sophie Waples:

> *"I think probably the most important thing is to really sit down, and go through everything that you need to complete, and make sure you actually understand the task. There's nothing more frustrating than when you're stressed, and you have so much work to do, and then you realise that you've been working for three hours on something, and you've actually taken*

the wrong step, or you actually don't understand what's being asked of you. If you are able to ask someone, to clarify on an assignment, or if you've been given a task at work, you should definitely take it because it's much better to ask a couple of extra questions, and save yourself, and whoever you're working for, hours, than to have to start all over again. That's probably my most immediate strategy, and just trying to keep cool, calm, and collected, as much as possible."

By breaking down big tasks into little tasks, I am able to not only quantify my achievements, but I feel a greater sense of accomplishment with each completed item. Feeling as though you are making strides with your work is paramount in managing your level of stress at the desk.

A cup of tea

Sometimes, a cup of tea solves everything. I'm not a coffee drinker, and thus can't speak of its benefits, but I am an avid fan of tea and find that it has a soothing effect on me.

"Elizabeth" and Jade Tyrrell are also advocates of tea to help you chill out.

"Elizabeth":

"Cup of tea break…It all depends on the context that you are in – where I am working currently, I have no problem doing that, but in the past, when I was working at a different firm, I felt really uncomfortable getting up from my desk, because I did not want to be perceived as slacking off, or anything like that, which is really problematic, but I think it is just about developing the confidence that if they do notice you are gone they are going to trust that you will be back within a reasonable time, and that they are not going to say anything much about it."

Jade Tyrrell:

"In terms of short-term strategies, I would always get up for a break. I think breaks are really underestimated in this sphere of life. A favourite little motto of mine is: 'a cup of tea solves everything'. So I think it's really important to treat yourself well and to relax and take breaks when you need to; listen to your body. I know that sounds pretty basic but it's an underappreciated message, and it can be quite a challenge in practical terms. I think taking breaks helps you to reset your mind so you can more successfully absorb information and process what you need to be thinking about. If you get to the point where you are becoming counterproductive you really just have to stop – even if it is just for five minutes. Take that break, find that balance, and when you come back to your work there's no doubt you'll come back to it with fresh eyes."

TWD Wellbeing Wisdom

There are a number of practical solutions that can be implemented – in accordance with Dr Fisher's approach – if ever you feel the need to take the pressure off while at work. Generally speaking, it doesn't matter too much which strategy you implement at any given time, so long as it temporarily takes you away – physically or emotionally – from whatever it is that is making you stressed.

Listed below are things to keep in mind:

- Briefly step away from the source of your stress (physically and metaphorically).
- Give yourself space to properly appreciate what you are facing. This is important because it will help you better understand the context of the situation.
- Allow yourself to feel overwhelmed, if need be. Don't shirk away from expressing your feelings. Give your feelings a "voice", but also manage them appropriately.
- Learn what triggers your depression and anxiety and what helps it. Once you have a firm grasp on these factors – discard the strategies that do not work, and focus on the ones that do!

Acknowledge how you feel by coordinating proper, helpful responses. For example, write a plan of attack and debrief with a colleague or confidant. Formulating a strategy not only gets the ball rolling, in regards to your designated task, it also gives you the confidence you need to achieve that goal. Here are some ways in which you can unwind and de-stress at your desk:

- Take a deep breath

  This is the simplest and most effect way to relax when you're at work or studying. It helps you clear your mind of frustration and tension, and helps you focus on a single point.

- Have a drink of water, tea or coffee

  When we get stuck into our work, we often forget to eat and drink. Rehydrating (albeit not something unhealthy) works wonders!

- Have a laugh

  As the old adage goes, laughter is the best medicine. Having a chuckle with a coworker or study partner can make anyone feel better about themselves and the situation they are in. It also provides much-needed perspective, at a time that you so often need it.

- Check your personal email account or social media pages

  There's no reason why you can't do this for a few minutes on your phone. See who has posted on your Facebook wall or tagged you in an Instagram photo. This is a great way to remember that you have a life outside of study and work.

- Have a ball ready to play with

  Whether it is a stress ball, tennis ball or cricket ball, I love having something handy to fiddle with when my concentration wanes. It's a great physical and mental outlet, and also helps you refocus on the task at hand.

- Put your headphones in

  We all have songs that make us feel better about ourselves. If you're feeling low at your desk, plug in your iPod and listen to some dulcet tones. Soon you'll be singing along to the beat and feeling better.

I have the utmost faith that you can and will complete your tasks by deadline. Remember, you are a lawyer because someone believed in you, and thought that you were strong enough, smart enough, and capable enough, to successfully perform the those tasks.

According to Orenstein, if people can manage their innermost emotions and feelings, they can achieve a measure of success (i.e. legal outcomes and personal satisfaction). The problem is that, we, lawyers, so often neglect to address our emotions and feelings, which negatively affects our wellbeing, causing us, in the process, to miss valuable opportunities to improve our "lawyering" skills. However, if we take the time to care for our own wellbeing, even for just five minutes, especially when we are feeling stressed at our desks, we will not only be more productive at work, we will also experience more joy in our lives.[43]

Graeme Cowan has discovered in research for his multiple books that these kinds of suggestions are well grounded because they allow an individual to strategically break up the monotony of their routine and better manage a working day.

> *"They [the above suggestions] are all about taking breaks, all about refreshing, rejuvenating, and all the evidence shows that people work most effectively when they pulse their energy and so they work in a concentrated way for 50 minutes and then take 10 to 15 minutes break doing something different, and all those things you mentioned, they are about taking breaks."*

43 Cowan, n 11, 19.

What is the best way for me to achieve a work/life balance?

I am, and always have been, a HUGE *Tintin* fan. My bedroom is cluttered with memorabilia, T-shirts and an entire set of comics. I also enjoy a handful of trashy reality TV shows like *Geordie Shore* and *The Bachelor.* The latter may occasionally be vacuous but, leaving aside the snobbery of such a mindset, that's exactly what I like about sitting down for an episode or two of trash TV. These shows help me unwind from the rigours of that day's work – in short, they help me escape.

For my more socially acceptable hobbies and interests, I play indoor soccer, mixed netball and cricket with old schoolmates. I recently bought myself a FitBit fitness tracker, and enjoy competing against myself in a healthy fashion in order to reach 10 kilometres in steps every day. In addition, I occasionally dabble in yoga and boot camp and I am part of a book club. Plus, I tend to binge-watch TV shows such as *House of Cards*,

Game of Thrones and *Suits*. I also try my best to read every night for at least half an hour before bed. Lastly, I typically go to the gym a few times a week – forcing myself onto the rowing machine and pumping myself up to lift weights (the weights thing is primarily for vanity's sake – the fact that there are health benefits involved is just a bonus).

What I find so great about these events and activities is that they are all mine – I chose them. I get pleasure out of them and they bring me immense physical and emotional benefits. Nobody has dictated what I should do in order to achieve my own weekly balance – I found them myself and I love them.

You need to do this too.

ALSA offered its own guidance on how best individual law students and lawyers can maintain a work/life balance, which encapsulates most of the advice espoused by the interviewees.

> *"Maintaining a work/life balance plays an important role in preventing burn out. It is not viable to centre our schedules solely around work or study commitments as this could lead to exhaustion, stress, distress, disillusionment, anxiety or depression. Getting an appropriate amount of sleep each night and ensuring you're recharged is not only important for maintaining a healthy lifestyle – it ensures that you are able to efficiently and effectively execute your work and study commitments.*
>
> *"Ensuring that students and lawyers are taking appropriate breaks, factoring in down-time, making time for hobbies, as well as rewarding their hard work – ensures that balance between work and life is achieved. Making time for life-related activities is not only good for your wellbeing but is also beneficial to your work life as it improves your work performance in the long term."*

We are constantly reminded through various online and sociocultural platforms about the benefits of yoga, body attack classes, paleo diets, and other such endeavours that add value, and potentially years, to our lives. There is no denying that these activities are indeed fantastic...for the people who want to do them, of course.

Activities that give you a balance outside of work are, in my mind, supposed to be for relaxation and wellbeing, not simply for the sake of checking off boxes or satisfying others. I have found that it is so much better to do something that you feel personally connected to, because ultimately you end up reaping greater emotional and spiritual rewards. That being said, there does need to be some consideration for your own health at the same time. For example, it is not wise to unwind after a hard day's work by eating a large block of chocolate. Although it may be tasty and make you feel temporarily better, there is a chance that you will feel bad later (i.e. calories, bloating, stomach upset, headache, moodiness, fatigue, etc.).

Thus, a balance between what you want and what is good for you is necessary!

To sum up, as long as you meet your own health halfway, there is no reason why your activities can't be pleasurable and have long-lasting effects.

Socialising

For Brendan O'Brien, touching base with old friends is a great way to get perspective and unwind. Friends can provide a level of perspective that you are not able to bring yourself – they know you better than most if not all people, and can bring you back to Earth when you need to be grounded!

> *"One of the things that gives me more pleasure outside of work is actually catching up with old friends. The older I get, the more I realise that they are often going through the same sorts of things throughout life, whether it's about work*

> *issues, the challenges of being a parent or just life in general. Being able to spend time with friends, and to really talk to them about things over a drink or dinner or whatever, gives me a great release."*

Like Brendan, "Eleanor Robinson" asserts that she profits from social interactions.

> *"Great supportive relationships are what help balance my schedule. I make sure that my relationships with my family and the people I love are always number one over work."*

I am very fortunate in that I have a wide range of friends from different areas and times of my life. The most meaningful network of friends I have, however, is my one from my alma mater, St Aloysius' College. At the time of writing, we are ten years out from high school but our bond is stronger than ever. As a group of approximately 20 guys, we catch up altogether about once a month, and I will see maybe four or five of them every week for dinner, drinks or even just a chat. Not everyone has such a friendship group in their life, and I know how lucky I am to have mine; they provide a balance in my life that I cannot get anywhere else. There's nothing I wouldn't do for those boys.

Volunteering

Rojda Dag, a fourth year law student at a Sydney-based university, has found that more altruistic pursuits, such as volunteering with children, provide her with an outlet that not only brings her joy, but also helps her develop as a person. Volunteering has also worked for me; not only does it allow you to focus on the needs of others and therefore help you reflect on your own, but it affords you professional and educational skills that you otherwise may not have been able to gain.

> *"I think volunteering is so much fun and so rewarding. I met some of my best friends through volunteering. They've all worked at organisations that help children, specifically young kids. They're so heart-warming, and they just bring you so much joy. I just love that when I volunteer I get all of these maternal instincts, and, yes, I want 30 children! I love all of the kids that I help. To me, that's a really healthy way to unwind. In addition, it benefits my law degree."*

Sports and outdoor activities

James Tobin, on the other hand, manages his health and wellbeing by including sports activities into his weekly plans. This is one of my favourite ways to balance out my schedule – it is fun, engaging and healthy. There are few things more satisfying than the physical rush from a solid workout! This is supported by research as well; a prominent symptom of depression is fatigue that emerges as a result of having an overactive mind but an underactive body.[44]

> *"I've always been a keen sportsperson. In fact, I played football up until about ten years ago. So I played football on Tuesday and Thursday nights, while in law school and while practising law. I also played on Saturdays. Even today, I still engage in touch rugby on a regular basis. Then, during the summer season, I'm a keen runner, so I do a lot of running to and from work, as a way to get fit and sort of kill two birds with one stone, as far as driving. In addition, I'm a keen cyclist, so I regularly ride to and from work. And I attend training sessions with a personal*

44 Cowan, n 11, 20.

trainer at the gym. All I can say is that there is no way I could work the hours I do if I didn't maintain my fitness, health and wellbeing the way I have."

"Robert James" supports this approach; he too makes a conscious effort to stay active and achieve a work/life balance.

"I go to the gym regularly. I find that I perform better at work when I'm more balanced, so if I go for a week without getting into the gym for a workout, I feel more sluggish, and less effective and precise at work than I would like to be. It's very important to be as balanced as you can be."

"Katherine" similarly relies on sporting endeavours, but also finds benefit in social pursuits.

"Exercise for me is number one. I find that when I let go and get physical exercise, or just exert myself physically, it is the best thing to relieve my stress. I have to say that busy periods of work is where I fall down and then I really notice because it affects my sleep patterns. So exercise is definitely my number one strategy to keep up to keep a work/life balance.

"Socialising is also crucial; I have a tendency to go underground, so to speak, if I'm in a stressful situation. But sometimes even if you don't really want to socialise, because of how busy you are, there are people that can bring you back into line and are outside the inner workings of your mind if you get stuck in that loop."

Academic endeavours

"John" takes a more intellectual approach to work/life balance. While this is not the first pursuit that would come to mind for me when trying to achieve a balance, I note that, on occasion, delving into academic interests – politics, world affairs, human rights, etc. – can be a great way to refocus your attention onto a different matter, and thus realign your priorities.

> *"I spend a lot of time browsing websites, such as the Human Rights Watch and Rescue International and* The New York Times. *I also spend time learning about the world – that's basically what I do at home. I've spent a lot of my spare time writing papers and essays for submission to journals, which is something that genuinely interests me, but I acknowledge that my head doesn't leave the law very often in this sphere."*

I get huge pleasure out of reading the papers or keeping up with my *TIME* magazine subscription. Delving into current affairs as a leisurely pursuit is a fantastic way for me to direct my intellectual and mental attention to something that I don't control…I can simply enjoy it.

Finding time for yourself

Sometimes, there doesn't even need to be a specific event or activity to create a work/life balance. In fact, it can be as simple as ensuring that a certain period of the day is reserved for your personal time. "Adelaide" knows this better than most.

> *"Day to day, I make morning a sort of sacred time. I think because you don't have to be in the office until a certain time, there is a window of a few hours to do what you want to do, if you can get up early enough, such as going out for a walk. Sometimes I do an exercise, or I practise meditation, or I just lie in bed awake. I just have a cup of tea and sit. That is my thing I do on a day-to-day level."*

I wholeheartedly agree with "Adelaide" on this front. Sometimes it is just important to simply sit and be with your thoughts and feelings. Ignoring them, or not giving them their due attention, is not a healthy strategy.

All of the abovementioned activity suggestions are fantastic ways to add value to your schedule and better shape your thoughts and feelings, so that you can progress through your day in a healthier and happier manner.

What if I give up an existing hobby?

It is also important to consider the work/life balance from the other perspective – what if you were involved in an activity that gave you pleasure, but could no longer continue it?

Lucinda Clarke provides insight into this scenario.

> *"I used to have such activities, but now I do less and less (some of this has to do with a change of jobs). Before I moved firms, I was singing at least once a week in a choir, and learning how to play the guitar. Since moving six months ago, I have had zero time for any of this. Music is a large part of my personality, so I am starting to become resentful of the lack of time/space for this in my life right now."*

If ever I miss my weekly indoor soccer or mixed netball games – due to illness, work commitments, or conflicts – I always regret it. Having those prearranged times to run around with friends, work up a sweat and exercise my latent competitive streak is so important to me; those games really are the among the highlights of my week. Without them, I feel lethargic, bored or even cranky. If you do have a hobby, do your utmost to keep it up. It might not always be possible, but don't slack off...it'll be worth it in the end.

So clearly it can work both ways. Take up a hobby, and you'll feel better – give up a hobby, and you may feel worse. The moral is to maintain your activities, because they will provide you with the work/life balance you need to be happy and successful.

It is important to understand that there is no hard or fast rule that determines what activities or hobbies you should pursue for your health and wellbeing. What works for others may not work for you, and vice versa. What really matters is that your exertions add value to your life. The best way for you to unwind is to find a physical, emotional and/or psychological balance with your professional duties (activities that will bring you joy, health, and stimulation). No one can determine that balance except for you...so choose wisely!

"Grace" sums work/life balance up perfectly:

> *"Do the things that you absolutely love. For me, it's going to the gym or dancing. I think that the things that make you feel like you are yourself, your true self, completely separated from work, are really important for managing your health and wellbeing."*

TWD Wellbeing Wisdom

With so many different options available that have the potential to provide a balance in your daily or weekly schedule, what are the best ones for you?

Only you can answer that question. As long as you adhere to the rule that activities should benefit you both physically and emotionally (including health and wellbeing), there should be no reason why you can't choose what you want to do.

Here are some tips to help you get started:

- Don't underestimate the value of social interactions with friends and family!
- Prioritise the people whom you care for the most, as well as those activities and items in your life that reap the most value for you.
- Experiment with different activities and hobbies until you find something that not only works for your schedule, but also is something that you enjoy.
- Don't limit yourself by comparing yourself to others – what works for them may not work for you!

Dr Fisher supports this:

> *"You've got to work out what actually generates a feeling of wellbeing for you. There are some people who do not get enjoyment or satisfaction from exercise, so they have got to ask themselves, 'What else can I do that does give me those positive feelings?'*
>
> *"That might be any number of intellectual or social interests, hobbies or activities that are not so physical."*

And, most importantly…

- MAKE TIME – DON'T FIND TIME!

If your hobby is a non-negotiable feature of your schedule, you exponentially increase your chances of maintain it, drawing benefit from it, and enjoying your personal and professional lifestyles.

I already have a busy schedule. If I take on a hobby, won't I become even more tired and stressed?

At face value, it may appear that you will increase your levels of stress and anxiety if you add another activity to what may be an already busy schedule. There just aren't enough hours in the day to do everything that needs to be done! The downtime that you do have typically ends up being reserved for sleep and relaxation – understandably so.

What I have found, however, is that certain hobbies and activities can bring joy and fun into your life that your schedule may otherwise not allow. They also provide physical and emotional energy that can be used in all areas of your life. For example, playing indoor soccer and mixed netball on Monday and Thursday nights gives me an opportunity to run around, work up a sweat, have fun with friends, be competitive, and feel like I have earned my sleep for that night. What I find, as a result, is that my batteries are recharged when I wake the next morning.

Graeme Cowan supports this, and notes that such inclusions to your schedule provide overwhelming benefit, rather than adding to the stress you may be experiencing.

> *"If it is something that you really like and is something to get involved in, it's likely to be good for you. And if you do things that are good for you, it does energise you and make you more resilient and robust; and so it's a way of recharging, it's a way of switching off when you do a hobby or an activity that you really, really like. And it's something that you know is good for you and builds your energy, builds your robustness, it's too important not to do it."*

Doing things you love and get value out of (when you're stressed) won't make things worse. It'll make things easier.

How to manage your timetable and combat wellbeing issues

Graeme and I aren't the only ones who have discovered that extracurricular activities will not, in fact, make you even more tired and stressed than you already are. Kate Taylor acknowledges this in discussing the profit reaped from her involvement in activities outside of work:

> *"I think it just helps me refocus on what my goals are and what's important to me and take a step back from it and reassess what I'm doing and why I'm doing it."*

In fact, interviewees praised the numerous benefits associated with individual and group hobbies. These individuals reported that hobbies and activities were especially beneficial for reducing school and workplace stress. According to "Katherine", participating in extracurricular activities provides you with a more balanced public persona.

> *"To be successful, you need to be a balanced person – I don't think you're ever going to get ahead if you are a one-dimensional person; having such activities will just add to your value as an employee."*

It can sometimes be understandable, even acceptable, for law students to underestimate just how important a work/life balance can be when you are overloaded with work. Jade Tyrrell recognised, upon graduation, that she needed to be stricter on herself when it came to achieving a work/life balance every week. Jade believed that this balance enhanced her productivity at work, and caused her to be happier outside of work.

> *"It's a practised skill, and I don't think I practised it well enough at the university, but now being in a full-time job, I force myself to exercise, I force myself to catch up with friends, and I force myself to read something that isn't work-related. Because that, as a whole, makes me happier, and a more holistic human being, and I feel doing things like that helps me in turn at work.*
>
> *"If I'm completely focused on work, and I find that I am completely ground down, that's just not good for my practice, in general."*

Of course, it is important to consider the timing of your hobbies and activities. For example, Sophie Waples admits making concessions during certain periods of the semester. To Sophie, it was important for her to partake in hobbies only at specific times of the year.

> *"I think you need to know when and how long you've got to get to your law assignments, and it's all about planning. If you know you've got an assignment due in three weeks, then you've got*

> *to arrange time, and make time to actually get started on it because otherwise, it won't get done. And it is really important to have other things outside of work and study because otherwise, you'll probably go a bit nuts."*

But even with consideration for your timetable, it would be fair to say that, sometimes, law students and young lawyers do not prioritise the activities that bring them personal satisfaction.

I know this because I used to do the same thing.

Frankly, there is a lot to be said about simply being kind to yourself and giving yourself the freedom to actually *live*. This does not mean throwing caution to the wind and ignoring your duties and responsibilities; rather, it simply means remembering that you are human. You are allowed to have fun, in whatever form that may take. "Adelaide" knows very well the importance of being kind and true to one's self.

> *"I think everyone is really different, and people deal with stress in many different ways, and that is why my advice would be to try and really analyse yourself, and understand what actually makes you stressed, and what your stresses are, because when you understand that type of stress, you are able to cope with it, that is when I think you can figure out whether you have the capacity to take on more activities.*
>
> *"And also plan exercises that fit in with your time, because we are all so busy. So the time constraints that we have, students and lawyers, mean that there is just not enough time, and we all know that feeling of being out at a party, but having a module of readings to do that hangs over your head, making you feel guilty, and as such you cannot be emotionally present at the party. I know that feeling. It's about time management, about self-awareness, and also about making peace with things.*
>
> *"I have experienced that feeling of guilt, when I was out, and could have been at home reading textbooks. But at some point, you just have to make peace with that, and you say, 'Yeah, I know I could be doing something else, but I'm not. I am here,*

and I'm going to be present here, and maybe it's stupid, but I am young, and I'm only going to do this once.'"

From an individual perspective, participating in an extracurricular activity is not going to make you more tired and stressed than you are already. In fact, it will actually benefit you by staving off these feelings and making you feel better about yourself. But there is more to consider than just how it will make you feel, and how it can assist your professional productivity. What these activities convey about you, as a professional, and as a person, can help you succeed in your personal life and in your work environment.

Terry McCabe spoke freely about the value of lawyers, who are well-rounded individuals, and why he, as an employer, would be more likely to hire a person who has passions outside of work.

> *"Whatever the activity is, whether it is soccer, knitting, mountain climbing, or studying Chinese, I would say not only that an individual should take up that activity, but that it is essential that they take up that activity.*
>
> *"One of the things that I look for in graduates who are coming to the firm, is what other activities have they been involved in apart from the study of law, because we're not one-dimensional people that are simply built to turn out advices, and deal with takeover codes in presentations. That gives us certain needs, like feelings that, professionally, we're doing good things. It also meets our financial needs, in that, we get paid, and there is within people, I think, a basic need to feel that they are contributing within the community by working in some way.*
>
> *"Australia's work ethic is deeply ingrained in society. But that is only one aspect of our souls, and to ignore all of our other needs, such as the need to be physically active and healthy, or the need to be able to get into some other pursuit that really*

engages you mentally, and gives you 'downtime' from the satiric magic of the takeover codes, I think is not just optional, it's essential."

I understand why some young lawyers might be hesitant to prioritise their extracurricular activities as a crucial part of their day or week, or why such people assume that by taking on another activity, it will somehow distract from their work and/or leave them with even less time for sleep and/or personal space.

But here is the principal of a large commercial firm saying that not only is it important for you to involve yourself in such activities (for your own benefit), but that he looks for those activities when he considers prospective employees.

Paying attention to your emotional and physical health, while studying or practising law, can also be professionally rewarding. Lloyd Wood, former president of the Law Students' Society at the University of Technology, Sydney, supports this, drawing on his experience as president of a leading law students' society:

"For me, extracurricular activities have been a hobby which has really helped. Being involved in extracurricular activities may not always relate to your law degree, but it can help through the connections and networks that you gain. You have the ability to meet new people, share study notes, help each other with assignments, and so on. Most of my successes would not have been possible without the connections I have made through extracurricular pursuits."

Therefore, what more motivation do you need to incorporate a healthy work/life balance into your life?

But even after that, there is another, more personal reason for getting involved in extracurricular activities.

"Peter":

"Find something that you enjoy or used to enjoy before you started working in law – something that you have forgotten, or

stopped doing, and go and do it again. Just forget about work for an hour or two, because it isn't the 'be all and end all' of your existence. I mean, anything could happen in life, and if you're just focused on work constantly, then you going to regret it. There are more people in your life that deserve your attention, and who are more important. This job gives you an ability to live by paying your bills and things, but it's not your life, and you shouldn't treat it like it is."

For most, if not all of us, family and friends are the most important things in our lives, if not the reason for our existence.

The people in my life, whom I love and care for deeply, are the reason I get out of bed in the mornings. They inspire me to do my best, personally and professionally, and they bring joy and meaning to my life. At this point, I strongly feel that everything I do, every project I work on, every activity I participate in, every action I take makes me a better person, so that I can, in turn, give back to the people in my life. I want to provide for them – financially, emotionally, and physically. And in order to do that, I need to be the best possible version of myself.

While I may love what I do, crudely speaking, it is just a means to an end – the end of which is to look after the people in my life. I am positive that many others feel the exact same way. There is a reason why it is called a "work/life balance". Work should be separate from your personal life! So enrich your life with as much fulfilment as possible.

TWD Wellbeing Wisdom

Dr Fisher provided a medical perspective on this issue (using the outlet of exercise as a key example) in discussing why having such additions to your timetable will ultimately be beneficial for you.

> *"We know that when people exercise regularly, many of them will be virtually become addicted. There are many reinforcers of habitual exercise. Endorphins and other chemicals, including serotonin, are released with exercise and the release of such chemicals may make you feel better.*
>
> *"Exercise first thing in the morning means that you start the day with a sense of achievement, get the body and brain ticking over, and have the opportunity of reflecting on the day ahead and planning how you will strike a balance between, work, relationships and leisure.*
>
> *"I think it is a fair comparison to make that, in effect, you are going into battle well-prepared by doing exercise first thing and it is one way of looking at working in a large law firm, or indeed in any form of legal practice that day to day is often enough like a battle. You may have some capacity to determine how well-equipped you are to make your way in that war zone."*

Utilising this, in addition to the opinions canvassed above, it is clear that the addition of hobbies or activities to your schedule won't compound your stress and anxiety, and that it will in fact add value to your being. That being said, you definitely need a strategy for managing your schedule.

Listed below are ways that you can add hobbies and/or activities into your daily or weekly routine (without them making you more tired than you already are):

- Choose an activity that you want to do – not what you think you should be doing.
- Plan your involvement in a hobby or activity by noting it in your

daily or weekly planner, so that you have a better chance of sticking to it.

- Make concessions, when necessary (i.e. exam period), but otherwise, try to stay motivated and participate in your chosen activity!
- Spend as much, or as little time, as you need to enjoy your activities and/or hobbies.
- Participate in that activity so long as it adds physical, emotional, intellectual or psychological value to your life outside of law.
- And, most importantly, remember that work does not have to be your life!

Do we have a tendency to self-medicate with alcohol?

Dr Fisher:

"I think it is a cultural commonality to use alcohol to wind down. It is potentially convivial and social, so one can see why people would be attracted to using these drugs.

"The downside to the use of alcohol and drugs can be the disinhibiting effect which can lead to professionally inappropriate behaviour like having sexual relations with a secretary or a married colleague, and then having to deal with the wash-up of that the following day or following weeks.

"Alcohol abuse will inevitably cause more harm than good and will adversely impact upon physical and mental health and imperil relationships with others as well as imperilling job security.

"The instant gratification obtained from the use of these things, at the end of the day, may absolutely not be worth the consequences."

Marie Jepson, of the Tristan Jepson Memorial Foundation (TJMF), is well informed on the causes and prevalence of depression in the legal industry, as TJMF have championed numerous studies on depression in law. As a result, she concedes that social and cultural factors contribute to the development of alcohol abuse and alcoholism.

According to Marie, this topic has been ignored or at least largely unexplored by researchers, psychologists, and scientists.

> "Courting the Blues *found that many men refuse to seek help preferring to 'self medicate' with alcohol. Alcohol often masks the symptoms of depression that impedes accurate diagnosis and delays appropriate treatment. In addition, the existing stigma of mental illness, together with a culture that endorses heavy drinking, leads many lawyers to deny they have a problem. They would prefer to have an alcohol-related problem rather than a diagnosis of depression or mental illness."*

This topic has, however, been considered in the United States, and the findings are troubling. Approximately 70 per cent of practising Washington State lawyers are likely to develop alcohol-related problems (i.e. alcoholism, cirrhosis of the liver, etc.), over the course of their lifetime (albeit at varying degrees), compared to just 13.7 per cent of the general population (non-lawyers).[45] Therefore, it is not a stretch to deduce that there are similar trends in Australia, New Zealand, and the United Kingdom.

Binge drinking, excessive drinking and alcoholism are by no means activities that are unique to the Australian legal community. In fact, it is common throughout Australian society. In all actuality, one could make a reasonable argument that law students and young lawyers partake in these types of

---

45 Connie J.A. Beck, Bruce D. Sales and G. Andrew H. Benjamin, "Lawyers Distress: Alcohol-related problems and other psychological concerns among a sample of practising lawyers" (1995–1996) 10 *Journal of Law and Health* 1.

damaging activities as a way to appear "normal" to the rest of society.

Orientation week, parties, law cruises, law pub crawls, club crawls, cocktail evenings, intervarsity activities, and conference galas, without a doubt, provide an extraordinary gamut of social activities that supply alcohol – lots of alcohol. And that's not including the external events put on by law firms during clerkship seasons. Graduate and other young lawyers are similarly inundated with such celebratory occasions – the most popular of which is drinks after work on a Friday night.

This by no means suggests that law students and young lawyers should give up drinking to excel in law school, or become a successful lawyer. In fact, to put forth such a proposition is preposterous, self-righteous and unreasonable. In all honesty, I appreciate and understand the social, cultural and emotional benefits associated with enjoying alcohol with friends and colleagues.

However, given the prevalence of depression, psychological distress, and anxiety in the legal community, law students and young lawyers should be wary of over-indulging in alcohol-fuelled activities, which, if left unattended, can perpetuate existing or underlying physical and mental health issues. Moreover, given the manner in which alcohol consumption is glorified as a regular leisurely pursuit, rather than a sporadic luxury, student events and after work drinks can easily take on a medicinal role. Alcohol can turn into a type of self-medication when used to cope with work and study-related concerns.

Excessive alcohol consumption can have the opposite effect of resolution. In fact, there are certain educational and/or vocational consequences associated with getting trapped within the party/social/alcohol culture. This is especially true for law students and lawyers, though of course can happen to anyone in any profession.

The goal of this chapter is to explore the social activities that some Australian law students and lawyers partake in. In fact, more often than not, these activities are merry and enjoyable, and should be applauded for being so; however, the potential for adverse effects should not be ignored or dismissed.

What effect does drinking have upon our wellbeing?

While conducting interviews for this book, I decided to inquire about the prevalence of excessive drinking in the law field. Do law students and young lawyers escape the rigours of study and practice by self-medicating with alcohol? Do law students and lawyers over-indulge in such pursuits? Or, is alcohol consumption (i.e. excessive drinking, alcohol abuse, binge drinking and alcoholism) just a part of the social and cultural environment that we, as Australians, live in? Most importantly, are there any dangers associated with excessive drinking when one is vulnerable to mental health problems, while in law school or practising law? And, finally, am I over-estimating the threat of excessive drinking in the legal profession?

Lloyd Wood, having been heavily involved in student politics and having simultaneously worked at a number of law firms, has been able to observe a variety of alcohol-related issues faced by law students and lawyers.

> *"I think it is perhaps an over-compensation by students saying, 'I study law and I need to prove that I'm social'. In my experience, at least, I've seen that students want to self-medicate with alcohol not because of their studies but rather just to show that they have a social life, despite the burdening time commitments*

of studying law. There are running jokes going on about this in some publications that our law students' society has released, for example saying that law students drink like fish. I think it's socially acceptable because there's an appreciation that we work so hard, and therefore we need a drink. It's tough to say that it's ingrained but at the same time I don't think it's frowned upon."

"Sunrise" is nearing the end of her law degree program. She has also been heavily involved in student societies and on-campus activities. The significant number of students exposed to this type of drinking culture led her to deduce that the relationship between law students and alcohol and its potential to serve as an enjoyable pastime should be reevaluated.

"I think drinking is a big thing. I'm not going to say to the extent that I know anyone who has alcohol problems...I mean, at least not in my circle of friends, but I see that alcohol is an escape. It is like, 'Oh my God, I can't wait to get wasted on Friday night; my life is so shit right now!' It's not like you turn to alcohol to enjoy it, you go to alcohol as a method of escape, and I think that's very dangerous."

The perspectives of Lloyd and "Sunrise" do not differ from what I witnessed, or even practised myself, when I was a law student. The anticipation for upcoming social events hosted by the law students' society or some other organisation were centred around the idea that this was an opportunity to "let your hair down", by way of partying, and having a good time with friends. And while one is able to enjoy a party, without having a few drinks, it was without a doubt a way to escape the strenuous and taxing environment of studying law. In essence, physiological inebriation can and often does lead to a temporary separation from real-life issues.

Why is this a bad thing?

Well, first it's important to reaffirm that alcohol

consumption is not a problem for everyone. However, it can be a problem for some. For those people, it can represent an alternative to speaking up about what is going on – an outlet through which they can deal with their issues, without actually having to deal with them. It is not unreasonable to suggest, further, that the more stressful a person's study or work is, the more likely they are to drink.

"J. McLeod":

> *"I think that with something like depression, at least personally, that's often the greatest hurdle, because in sharing it with someone you've got to actually confront that there's an issue. I felt ashamed when I had to do it."*

But how does a problem with alcohol arise?

Kate Taylor:

> *"Obviously the drinking culture among law students is quite well known. And, it is probably exacerbated by...first you've got law camp, where students are discreetly told to bring their own alcohol, and told that the party is going to be big and wild. From day one it's kind of embedded in your mind that that's the best way to unwind. And that continues at a lot of the arranged social events – in fact, one of the big promotional pushes in attracting student interest is that there's alcohol at the event, even if it's a speaker seminar.*
>
> *"And that seems to be something that's definitely a part of the law school culture. I mean, despite the well-known health effects of drinking, I've found that where the law communities are quite small, there's a lot of social repercussions to being at an event or not being at an event, and being in those social circles; which I guess adds another pressure to law school."*

As a result, we can now establish that alcohol abuse has the capacity to become a cultural norm while in law school. It also has the propensity to mask the issues that law students face while in their law degree program.

Can these issues manifest once a person is working in law too?

According to Nick Edwards, it depends on the situation and the person. However, this does not necessarily have to be a bad thing. In other words, if a person chooses this avenue to unwind, it is still better than not finding time to relax and enjoy life.

> *"I think that it's very much a problem in the legal fraternity, but abuse of alcohol is probably more of a reflection of stress. Obviously, there is illicit drug use, and things like that happen; but I don't think necessarily that it's widespread. The bigger problem is people actually not winding down. I think that would be more of a concern for me. Binge drinking is not great, but at least then people are winding down, and not thinking about work on that level. But a bigger problem for my mind would be the inability of people to actually wind down, to leave work at the doorstep when they go home."*

Maxine Evers takes a slightly different approach, discussing the potential for such a practice to become culturally ingrained, whether it be at law school or in legal practice.

> *"I think it's very much the culture, and I've certainly been a part of that, of a reward for a hard week's work, and it's very much around that's how you might celebrate a success in litigation, or the stitching up of a deal, or just the sheer hours, challenges, and problems that you've experienced, so that seems to be the way you would relax and celebrate. However, it certainly wasn't, when I was in practice, considered that every Friday after work that you'd go out and play lawn balls, or you'd go for a walk, or you might even go to have a meal, or have a game of tennis or something. It's all very much about having drinks in the boardroom.*
>
> *"Well, it becomes just part of that culture, so it then becomes something that is embedded in what lawyers do, and it's about*

> *finishing every big case, or every big deal, or every hard day with a drink, and any non-legal occasion where work is not being done – outside conferences, or outside court appearances, or outside meetings – the only other way of getting together is having a drink."*

For Brendan O'Brien, such recreational activities were never a method of escapism for him personally; however, he does note that they are common practices for those in stressful situations.

> *"If you've got a big project going on at work, or you've been busy with a lot of cases, going out on a Friday night and drinking a lot might seem like the best way to relax and unwind. I certainly used to go out drinking with colleagues, particularly before I had children, but I don't think I ever really did it as a way of dealing with work issues. If drinking, or taking drugs, is a way of dealing with whatever is going on in your work, then that's a problem that should be addressed."*

Of course, everything must be done in moderation. Alcohol abuse can get out of hand regardless of whether you are a lawyer or not. While having a few drinks can be a great way to unwind and take the pressure off, it must not become *the* way that you or anyone else de-stresses after a hard day of law study or practice.

One of the interviewees – a senior lawyer in a large Australian commercial law firm – talked about this, but asked to be referred to as "Lawyer#32", so as to protect the individual being discussed in the following quote.

> *"In a recent episode, one of my colleagues very sadly departed the firm after he'd been struggling with, I would say, a mental illness for some time, and that had also then crept into the form of addiction. He'd become an alcoholic, and he had been battling with those demons for some time. I understand he's put himself into some serious rehab in trying to overcome those demons, but a combination of an addictive personality, a high-stress situation, I've no doubt that the combination of those*

> *elements can be a cocktail for disaster, and that's been very sad to watch."*

What happened to this anonymous senior lawyer's colleague could, of course, happen to anyone in any industry. This book focuses on the increased risk of developing psychological distress, anxiety and depression when in law school or practising law. Although, it is still important to note that alcohol can be a contributing factor in these conditions.

Marie Jepson:

> *"Self-medicating with alcohol is a very acceptable means of relaxing and making contact with people. Certainly the barristers will tell you, you can go meet your clients, or the people, who will provide your clients, over a drink, and then when you win a case, you also celebrate. If you lose a case, you then need to commiserate, but it's all done with alcohol. And increasingly what you hear is that people under stress are using drugs.*
>
> *"Firstly, it masks the symptoms of their illness, and their stress. Alcohol actually is a depressant, so it seems to initially make you feel better, and then there comes the downer, so that on top of the fact that you are struggling, and may have the symptoms of depression and anxiety, you're actually making them worse, and prolonging the time till you seek help. The biggest factor in stress reduction that gets little attention is adequate sleep. And there is a huge gap between sufficient rest, and the next factor that they consider, so having little sleep, burning the candle at both ends, and doing it on a prolonged basis cannot be remedied by lots of exercise, eating healthily, or being in a fun run or anything like that. Your body needs a certain amount of sleep, and that would be the first thing that I would say that needs to be prioritised. You function much better when you are rested. It's considered torture to deprive people of sleep, so people need adequate sleep in order to perform."*

young legal professionals need to be aware of this. ıtimately, it will come down to your good judgement and ommon sense.

Professor McKeough:

> *"I think you have to rely on healthy drinking limits, most people exceed them most of the time and there are some online instruments which help people determine how healthy they are and how much they're drinking, so I direct someone to an online resource that will give them a snapshot of whether or not what they're doing is appropriate."*

TWD Wellbeing Wisdom

Alcohol use and abuse is a proven indicator of negative wellbeing, and is associated with decreased internal motivation and decreased experiences of autonomy, relatedness and competence.[46] So by all means, enjoy a night out with your friends when you feel like it. No one is suggesting that you ignore this socio-cultural activity, especially on the occasions in which unwinding with colleagues is appropriate.

However, I personally advise that you bear in mind the following:

- You are more susceptible to issues of wellbeing than those outside of the legal profession. Therefore, it is important for you to drink in moderation whenever you choose to do so.
- Alcohol consumption/abuse is *not* the answer when it comes to seeking a balance in your life. As you will discover in other chapters of this book, there is a plethora of events and activities for you to get involved in so that you can achieve balance in your life and unwind from the stresses of law.
- It is crucial to know your limits and capacities – the idea of "work hard, play hard" is outdated and dangerous. Have a good time but don't ever feel the need to write yourself off.
- Be clear in your motivation for consuming alcohol: having fun with friends and colleagues is fine, but if you are there to escape from the rigours of your study or work, then you're there for the wrong reason.

Dr Fisher offers practical, authoritative advice to reinforce my own when it comes to occasional or even habitual use of alcohol has a stress-reliever.

46 Krieger and Sheldon, n 2, 615.

think the starting point with so-called recreational 'drugs and lcohol' is understanding that they can and often do damage or destroy the body's cells, both in the brain and in the body tissue generally, including the liver.

"Alcohol firstly anaesthetises cells, and then pickles them.

"Drugs and alcohol are not necessary for our survival and they are not obligatory in a social context.

"As a civilised, mature and healthy adult, you should stop and think twice about doing things that injure your mental and physical functioning."*

What have other people experienced? How do I know I'm not alone?

Law students and young lawyers tend to be hesitant about asking for help, if or when they face health problems. In fact, young legal professionals often feel that they either are responsible for or should be able to resolve their own issues.

We previously discussed the competitiveness among law students and young lawyers; however, pride, for lack of a better word, may be another factor that influences a person's decision to not seek help. They may not want to appear weak in front of friends, colleagues and/or classmates. Therefore, it is important that the concept of asking for help be normalised, at issues can be dealt with as early as possible.[47]

aving gotten this far through the book, you already know at happened to me. My story by itself gives rise to the idea t if you, the reader, are experiencing any health problems, u are not alone. I have been there too, and as a result I am here with you through whatever you are going through.

I am always uplifted and inspired whenever I see legal professionals in *Lawyers Weekly* talk about their struggles with depression and how they were able to come back from the brink. These types of meaningful, heartfelt stories help fight the stigma surrounding being a legal professional and having depression. But what I have never seen, and have longed to see, is a platform that takes the experiences of legal professionals who have suffered health problems and documents them in one place. This book aims to do just that.

Throughout the chapters, nearly 50 junior and senior legal professionals have detailed their experiences with psychological distress, anxiety and/or depression. They have also shared what they have seen in their friends, colleagues and classmates. This chapter presents an even deeper snapshot of what those interviewees have experienced and/or witnessed.

If you're a young legal professional who suffers from depression, or if you are concerned about how to best look after yourself and those around you, the ensuing interview excerpts will give insight on how you can aid your own recovery. In fact, individuals with issues of psychological distress, anxiety and depression exhibit courage when they share their health problems with others. Why do they do that? To let you know that you are not alone.

47 Vines, n 32.

What have our TWD Champions experienced?

Gavin Ingram:

> *"I thought it was just me. I thought I was the only person on the planet who felt this way because I saw everyone else around me working at 120 per cent. I thought this was just me. I didn't get the sense that this was a broader problem."*

"Elizabeth":

> *"I often experience dark periods, and they are like weights on my chest. I feel very vulnerable, very insecure. I also find myself being very teary, and very critical of myself (i.e. taking comments much more critically, than I'm sure they were intended to be). I also, as you can probably see, have a tendency to pick at my skin around my fingers, which I've heard is a common sign of depression. Furthermore, I find that my depression arises when I am particularly stressed."*

Luke Furness:

> *"I haven't experienced depression, and I say that I haven't because I know there are special medical definitions when it comes to anxiety and depression. I'm not a psychologist, but I've definitely had periods of being very down, feelings of having a complete lack of self-confidence – thinking that law isn't for me, thinking that I was stupid, or that I was the only one, who couldn't do a task, and that sort of thing. But I know that there are people who have had really bad experiences, so I'll never have to say that I was diagnosed with anything like that."*

"J. McLeod":

> *"I kind of just didn't really address [the issues that were accumulating], and I didn't really communicate with tutors or people until someone forced me to and said that I wasn't fooling anybody…kind of like forced me to 'fess up to what was wrong. I did feel hypocritical because I'm aware that speaking about university first, that there are quite a wealth of support*

mechanisms that I could have drawn upon. I think the reason I didn't was because I just didn't want to accept that maybe it was an ongoing or actual issue that I was facing that I couldn't get myself out of."

Clary Castrission:

"I don't know if there's a label for it, but I do remember I was in third or fourth year, and I was in a pretty dark place, but I didn't know what it was. That was eight or nine years ago and mental health wasn't as big as an issue at that time, so it didn't really occur to me to go and speak to a mental health professional about it. I did go to the university counsellor once, just to get a check in, and she kind of just said, 'What you're feeling is normal and not a problem,' and maybe that reassurance helped me. That being said, I don't know if it was law that caused that or whether it was the five-year relationship that at that time was starting to unwind a bit, so that could have had an effect. It was also after I'd started my company and I'd been spending a lot of time in India.

"I think I probably underestimated the psychological effect the villages were having on me back at that time, because I'd be spending a lot of time by myself in the village, and it was very lonely. Coming back into a Sydney environment, the two worlds collided. I wouldn't be able to identify what caused that darkness, whether it was law, the unwinding relationship, the company, I'm not sure. But yeah, I certainly did go through a period of it."

What have our TWD Champions witnessed in others?

Matthew Littlejohn:

"I certainly knew a couple of people at university who had issues with substance abuse, mainly alcohol, to a reasonably serious level. The law school culture also added to these issues and caused its own problems. One student, who had stayed up all night doing a 24-hour take-home exam, hadn't slept for 24

hours, 30 hours, whatever, had a few drinks at the university bar in the afternoon and then tried to drive home. He hit a pole, smashed up his car. He was lucky; he managed to walk away. But it was a terrible situation for him to be in and could easily have been much worse. In terms of issues in the workplace, my firm regularly runs vicarious trauma training, and they have a part where we are encouraged to talk about reactions we've had to traumatic client situations.

"At the last training session, there were some senior people in the room who were able to get up and share that they had been particularly affected by cases they'd dealt with, which was really good to see. It's a good example that they can talk about it and acknowledge that clients and work situations can have a material impact on you, because as a junior lawyer you haven't got that experience yet and it can seem very overwhelming. It makes the senior lawyers and partners more approachable, knowing that they aren't immune, and that you're not expected to be either."

"Louise":

"I have about ten close friends that are lawyers, I think two definitely have depression, and probably a couple more after that, so it is fairly prevalent."

Paul Redmond:

"One of my classmates from law school suffered a very serious depressive episode following a chronic fatigue incident about 20 years ago which forced him to leave a large corporate law firm. He had been suffering from depression for many years. I was very close to him, so it was very disappointing. In terms of law students, yes, you do see the effects. I have had a law student who cut her wrists in my office, while I was on the phone.

"She was obviously depressed. She had come to see me about an alternative exam. She has a history of cutting herself. If you work with young people, at a very sensitive and stressful time in their lives, which leads into their professional adult lives, of course, depression is going to be a big thing."

"Palm Tree":

> *"I had one friend who was a really smart guy. He would study and do his assignments, but he would also become so anxious about his grades that at the end of the day, he wouldn't submit the assignments. Even though they were completed, he would be so upset, or so depressed and anxious, that he just couldn't physically submit the assignments. He applied for an extension, and then spent two weeks editing the assignments. He then just wouldn't submit them at the end of the two weeks. Unfortunately at the end of his program, he had failed so many classes; he dropped out of law school."*

Nathan Kennedy:

> *"I have seen others who have had mental health problems. I have had people in my office in tears...I think you have to remember that you and your health are the most important things."*

Maxine Evers:

> *"In law school you see students who are studying or working, and you physically see some change in them – you can tell that they don't look well, they look tired, they look pale, they had lost weight, their eyes are not clear – they just didn't look as young as they normally did. If you were familiar with their workloads and/or their study loads, then you could connect the dots, and say, 'The changes had something to do with the work that they were doing.'"*

TWD Wellbeing Wisdom

The 12 preceding excerpts are incredibly candid and, in instances, heartbreaking. The transparency and starkness of these shared experiences make it all the more important that you take heed of the following suggestions:

- Whatever you feel or experience is, in all likelihood, something that another person has already experienced. Take heart in the fact that you can overcome your issues, just as others have overcome theirs.
- Every person who was interviewed for this book is currently thriving in his/her professional life, despite the enormity of what he or she experienced or witnessed. Remember: No matter how bad things get, there is always a light at the end of the tunnel!
- There are practical solutions for all of the scenarios listed above... health issues can be managed with proper application and consideration.

Later in this book is a chapter on available resources that you can use if ever you feel the need for assistance beyond what you, or your loved ones, can provide for you.

All law students and young lawyers grappling with wellbeing issues should heed the words of Justice Shane Marshall of the Federal Court of Australia who spoke at the Wellness for Law Network's annual 2015 conference:

> *"The most significant matter for law students, academics and practitioners to know about mental health (and judges too for that matter) is that you are not alone, and almost certainly there will be someone who has experienced exactly what you have experienced. Understanding that you are not alone, and that there are people who have risen to high levels in the legal profession or academy, and who have struggled with issues that you too have struggled with should be a source of great encouragement.*

"Successful people who have battled mental distress include Mark Twain, Theodore Roosevelt, Abraham Lincoln, Sir Winston Churchill, Geoff Gallop, Andrew Robb, Catherine Zeta Jones and Madonna.

"Knowing that they are not alone, together with changes to law school curriculum, can provide a greater focus on mental wellbeing, development of soft skills, and an integrated attitude to the law. These actions can only help improve the overall health of law students and practitioners."[48]

Never doubt that you have the capacity to affect meaningful change and to lead a successful law career, even if you find yourself suffering from psychological distress, anxiety or depression. These experiences can provide you with a great deal of perspective and insight, which will be invaluable for your personal and professional development.

There are thousands of people, in addition to the celebrities named above, who have overcome mental health issues and achieved greatness in their lives, many of whom are successful lawyers. There is no reason why you can't be one of them.

---

48 Justice Shane Marshall, "Depression: an issue in the study of law" (Speech delivered at the Wellness Forum for Law Annual Conference 2015, The Australian National University, 6 February 2015) <http://www.fedcourt.gov.au/__data/assets/pdf_file/0004/26608/Marshall-J-201502.pdf>

How can I help friends, colleagues or classmates who have such health issues?

Lauren Fitzpatrick:

"From what I've experienced at law school, there are a lot of avenues to assist people, whether it be mentoring programs, counselling and other support networks, but I also think that the main people that should really assist the ill person are those on the frontline, such as their family and friends. They are the people who will really notice more than others, who don't have that one-on-one interaction and don't really know them personally. Family and friends are the main people who need to stand up and take an active role."

Mental health issues within the legal profession do not only affect individuals, they also affect communities.[49] Therefore, acknowledging the needs of everyone will ultimately ensure the health and wellbeing of law students and young lawyers.

We, as individuals, need to notice when our friends, colleagues, family members, acquaintances, love interests, and classmates are unwell.

This chapter looks at the ways in which our interviewees have assisted, and will continue to assist, those around them (i.e. the attempts and the results). It also emphasises the importance of casting a wider net when managing the health and wellbeing of yourself and others. Lauren notes in the above comment that it is the people closest to you that have the greatest access to your innermost thoughts and feelings; as such, they are best able to assist you when you need help. By the same token, you are also well positioned to help the people in your life.

"Palm Tree":

> *"If you recognise the symptoms of depression in a friend, there's nothing wrong with approaching him or her in confidence and talking to him or her about it. It is important to let that person know that it's okay and that you're there to help."*

What are the ways to show support to those around me?

The importance of self-care in conjunction with care for others is something that ALSA strongly advocates.

> *"The best way to look after those around you and recognise signs of depression in your friends, colleagues or classmates is to talk*

49 Dr Sharon Medlow, Dr Norman J. Kelk and Professor Ian B. Hickie, "Depression and the Law: Experiences of Australian Barristers and Solicitors" (2011) 33 *Sydney Law Review* 794.

to them and if you notice something that concerns you ask, 'Are you okay?' ALSA is a supporter of R U OK? Day and encourages its affiliate societies to hold events around this time to highlight the importance of communication and openness when it comes to mental health. ALSA also strongly endorses the view that in order to be able to look after peers, friends, colleagues or even clients, one must be taking adequate care of themselves. This includes seeking help, being able to openly discuss any issues and also pacing oneself and taking preventative precautions. As such, we encourage people to lead by example. While students and young lawyers are urged to make themselves available when someone is in need of support – or someone to talk to – they are also reminded to know their own limits when helping someone else. Sometimes the best thing you can do is refer a friend, classmate or colleague to someone more experienced or to a support service. Trying to assist someone when you are not fully equipped places unnecessary stress on you, and may ultimately cause more harm than good."

As such, how can we effectively help those around us, as well as ourselves? Gavin Ingram has been able to reach colleagues by sharing his own personal experiences with mental illness.

"When I come across those people, I try and be as supportive as I can be; I open up and tell them about my story, and try to give people comfort in saying that it's not a life sentence. There's support out there and there's help available. Probably the first and hardest step is just being willing to talk about it. There's nothing to be ashamed of. I mean, we all get through it, we all continue to go on and do great things. And it's just making sure that once you recognise it and accept it, you can seek the appropriate treatment for it. Treatment and recovery will differ from person to person."

This has also been the experience of Aimee Riley, who draws inspiration from the shared experience of herself and those whom she cares about.

"I get comfort from knowing that some of my friends are going

through the exact same thing."

The approaches of both Gavin and Aimee emphasise one of the major cornerstones of this book, which is to assure others that they can overcome their issues. Therefore, the interviewees' experiences are invaluable for health and happiness.

One of the most practical forms of assistance I received when I was unwell was from friends and mentors who shared their own experiences of mental illness with me. Listening to someone else's tale makes you feel less alone, and it also provides you with an in-depth perspective that you may not have had prior to those conversations. Simply put, those discussions helped me determine where I wanted to be (physically and emotionally), once I recovered from my depression. And, as a result, I was left with an extraordinary feeling of empowerment.

The simplest action, such as asking a person how he or she is feeling can make an enormous difference in that person's life. You may not realise it, but taking time out of your own day to acknowledge and focus on someone else benefits your own mental health as well as providing comfort to someone else who may be experiencing the same things you are. Brendan O'Brien, another senior lawyer, discovered an effective way to help others.

> *"I remember asking a junior lawyer one day how she was going and she actually thanked me and told me how she was feeling. She was okay, but I think it was more the fact that someone had just asked. That was a while ago but I always think about it. It's a question that should be asked more often and it doesn't get asked often enough I think. If you don't ask the question, you won't find out."*

It is, of course, possible that reaching out to the person next to you will not elicit a productive response. Given the sensitive nature of the topic at hand, the instinct to remain closed off is perfectly understandable, and even reasonable, when faced with the friendliest or hospitable of gestures. However, it is important to remember that positive actions, even if they do not reap benefits at the moment, can assure someone that there are people who are willing and able to help him or her. So maybe the next time you ask someone how he or she is feeling, the recipient may just decide to confide in you.

Never underestimate the value of asking someone how he or she is doing.

"Gillian", who works as a judge's associate and asked not to be named, experienced a stirring testimony from a senior colleague that had a powerful effect on her life.

> *"During one of my clerkships, a senior partner gave a speech on mental health, within the workplace. The senior partner said, 'I've suffered from depression.' He shared this information in front of the whole firm. He went on to say that he took time off from work and sought counselling. The partner's admission was probably one of the most inspiring testimonies that I had ever heard. He also reported that one in three lawyers suffer from a mental illness like depression and/or anxiety. He continued, 'Well, because I know that one in three lawyers suffer from mental illness, I'm not going to excuse our law firm from this statistic. Why? Well, because I, myself, have also suffered from mental health issues.'*
>
> *"That was a huge admission for the senior partner to make in front of the whole firm. I only wish that more workplaces were open to having similar forums on mental health, but unfortunately, it is still perceived as a 'weakness'. In fact, employers want workers who can perform like machines,*

> *they don't, however, want workers who have to take sick days because it affects the firm."*

Transparent and intimate discussions among close friends are paramount for your health and wellbeing. There is something comforting about acknowledging or learning that there are others out there who suffer from or have experienced the same issues as you. Crudely speaking, it is reassuring to know that you are not some kind of freak or unnatural being.

I have a handful of friends from law school at UTS whom I know seek and find comfort in talking to me about their health and wellbeing issues. This comfort comes not from the idea that I am anyone special in the legal field (I'm not), but from the fact that I am their peer. I graduated ahead of some of them, and as such they may see my experience as a pathway that they can learn from. In these instances, where friends call on me for assistance, I am only too happy to help. Without help from friends and colleagues, I would never be able to pass on anecdotes to others. Troy Douglas agrees; he feels strongly that talking to friends is a useful alternative treatment approach to treating psychological distress, depression and anxiety. He recommends that you share your issues and concerns with those in your inner circle.

> *"I think that there needs to be more 'openness'. Thankfully, I was fortunate enough to have really open friendships, and people in my life that I could share my stresses with."*

This type of care and support should also extend to those who you may not be close to. Matthew Littlejohn discussed how important it is to look out for those around you, even if you are healthy and issue-free.

> *"You may be happy and healthy, but what about the person next door, you know, in the next office? Young lawyers are often in a graduate group of five to ten people, and although you may be handling your condition quite well, if there's nine others in your group, there is a good chance that at least one person*

is not handling it as well as you are. Therefore, being able to recognise when someone is struggling helps him or her handle what he or she is going through. And knowing what to do and what to look for is just as important as looking after yourself."

Looking after someone else not only requires minimal effort, but it also has the ability to help that person accomplish his or her goals. "Monty", whom I perceive to be someone who often goes beyond the call of duty and never just does the supposed minimum, discussed how small gestures could make a world of difference in someone's life.

"I've seen colleagues get extremely stressed at work, work late nights and lose themselves in the job. In those circumstances and if it is someone I know, if it's a peer, I may say 'let's grab coffee' or ask them 'how are you going?', that sort of thing."

Such care for a friend or colleague is all about the symbolic gesture in a lot of cases. A simple text message or email can lift a person's spirits; leaving flowers or chocolates on someone's desk can bring a smile to their face; including a person in your lunch plans can save them from extended periods of loneliness on any given day. Such gestures cost you nothing, and in most cases, they will be things that you would want to do anyway. So get out there and extend a helping hand!

It is also important to instil a level of confidence and comfort in someone who wants to confide in you. If you have found it useful to share your issues and concerns with friends, share this tip with others, because what works for you may also work for someone else. According to Sarah Beth, in-depth discussions with friends are essential for providing support and resources to someone in need.

"It makes a big difference to be able to talk to your friends about your issues. It is important to recharge and invest in your own 'time out'. When your days are centred on working on large matters, managing expectations and delivering results, it is important to shift perspective and connect – this will also

help you perform better at work as you have invested in resting the mind and potentially will have engaged different thinking patterns. Meeting up with supportive friends and family is not only enriching, it also helps shift you from the work-centred mindset concerned with obsessing over what comes next, and what needs to be done."

At the height of my ill health, every member of my immediate family was either overseas or interstate. As such, my close friends became my substitute family. On so many occasions during those months, I was able to pour out my heart to a small group of friends whom I knew would always respond with kindness, empathy, constructive guidance, and even a verbal ass-kicking (if that's what I needed). As was always the case, I was better at writing my thoughts and feelings down rather than saying them out loud. As such, my friends would often get text messages, emails or Facebook posts in the dead of night. Thankfully, they never failed to step up and wrap a literal or proverbial arm around my shoulder.

These friends saved me in so many ways. Angus, Michael, Codie, Jack, Nicole, Isha, Alice and Natalie are all extraordinarily special people, and I feel that no quantum of gratitude I show will ever suffice. Given the way in which my friends took care of me, I will always want to go above and beyond to help out others.

"J. McLeod" believes that transparent, vulnerable discussions with close friends and relatives help you better recognise and empathise with other people's struggles. And, as a result, you are better able assure those in need that they are not alone.

"Thankfully, I have not had to address my mental health issues in a formal context, when I didn't want to. I prefer, instead, to chat with friends, who have said, 'Well, I've experienced that too', or 'My brother had the same thing'. Just being able to discuss my issues in a quiet, relaxed setting has been tremendously beneficial for me."

Finally, it can be argued that stepping up to help somebody else can have positive flow-on effects for your own person and wellbeing. Graeme Cowan discussed this, in reference to the importance of volunteering for those within your immediate and wider community.

> *"When people volunteer, there's such a thing as helper's high and people that do volunteer, they live longer, they're healthier, and they also are more engaged in their work and enjoy their work more. And it is an incredibly good thing for staying in a positive mood."*

Of course, many of us will help those around us without any consideration for what we can personally reap from the situation. Altruism does not work like that. However, the idea that it will also be beneficial for us in turn is certainly not something to be passed up!

TWD Wellbeing Wisdom

Managing your own health and happiness is a task in itself, but even just small contributions can help others, and possibly even yourself.

Bear in mind the following so that you can better help those around you:

- Loved ones (friends, family and mentors) are best placed to help someone in need. Give that person the freedom and comfort to open up to you, so that you can assist constructively. It is so much scarier to open up to strangers or in formal settings…so allow them to open up to you.
- Unwell people draw inspiration from shared experiences and anecdotes; encourage openness by vocalising your own struggles where applicable, so as to aid the wellbeing of others.
- No gesture goes unnoticed or unappreciated – offer any level of help or support that you can…you never know what effect it could have!
- Offer the best advice you can depending on the scenario. Sometimes, people need reassurance and hand-holding, and at other times, they need to be lectured to. Judge the situation and respond accordingly. Don't be afraid to be stern; if they are a loved one, they will appreciate where you are coming from.
- Only ever suggest what is in the best interests of a person's health and wellbeing; everything else is secondary.
- If ever you feel frustrated at the lack of progress someone may be making, please have patience. Their struggle is real, and it is incapacitating at times. Let them go at a pace that suits them, so long as they are doing what is best for their wellbeing.
- DON'T EVER GIVE UP ON SOMEONE. You wouldn't want them to give up on you.

Dr Fisher:

"You first need to recognise that, often enough, a problem

shared is a problem halved. We have choices of either avoiding getting involved in other people's problems or we find that a few words and a listening ear makes a huge difference to that individual. It can also make the environment in which you are working more civilised.

"These are ethical and philosophical concepts which I believe should characterise good work places. So for more senior lawyers and managing partners, making it your business to understand a bit more about what is going on with colleagues' lives, observing their functioning in the workplace, and being aware of the characteristics of the common mental illnesses is something which can make a big difference."

What makes law such an important profession in our society, and how can I help effect meaningful change?

I am a big believer in the importance of law in modern society. My conviction was largely inspired by Sir Gerard Brennan, who, over the course of his judicial career, encouraged lawyers to demonstrate a capacity to serve those around them.

> *"Communities will be better and stronger because of the contributions lawyers make to them. Moreover, a long and satisfying life in the law is not merely assured by the success that flows from professional expertise, or the financial rewards associated with this career. It is, however, assured by the service*

that lawyers provide to others."[50]

Law is, at its core, an altruistic profession. It has a tremendous influence over the day-to-day functions in society; without the rule of law, society would be anarchistic. It would be – literally and metaphorically – lawless. Because of the special skills, knowledge and expertise afforded to legal professionals, they are in a unique position to influence the operational and functional details within communities. Without doubt, lawyers have a duty to serve people to the best of their abilities.

Furthermore, over the course of my (admittedly so far short) legal career, I have found that the most emotionally and professionally rewarding experiences stem from tasks that help others and the community in general.

I believe that law students and young lawyers will value the study and practice of law in a more meaningful manner if they are able to comprehend the usefulness and purpose of its presence in their lives. It is important to note that this goes beyond a typical 9-to-5 job, which is often required for lawyers. Understanding the law's place in communities can go a long way in achieving this initiative.

But what does an appreciation for law have to do with your own health and wellbeing? Well, if you suffer from psychological distress, anxiety and/or depression, it can adversely affect the people around you. This is not a criticism of you or anyone else; it is simply the reality of the situation sometimes.

It is also important to understand that as a young legal professional, you have skills, knowledge and expertise that the majority of people do not have; therefore, you are able to make tangible contributions in society. This is especially true

50 Sir Gerard Brennan, "Keynote Address" (Speech delivered at UTS Brennan Justice and Leadership Program Awards Night 2013, University of Technology, Sydney, 26 September 2013)

if you make a genuine effort towards that pursuit. Understand that your work is uplifting. In fact, the services you provide can positively affect your wellbeing and motivate you to keep going, even when you don't want to.

The importance of law in our society

Towards the end of the interviews for this book, I asked interviewees why they believe law is an important vocation in modern Australian society (assuming that they did hold this view). We also discussed the causes and effects of depression, along with traditional and alternative treatment options. Given the bleak nature of those conversations when considered in full, I would have easily forgiven the interviewees if they had espoused cynicism, suspicion and/ or scepticism when asked the question as to why law is so important in day-to-day Australian society.

Yet I was blown away by the interviewees' passionate views on law. And although social, cultural, environmental, and health problems (i.e. psychological distress, depression, and anxiety) exist in law school and in the legal field, most legal professionals still maintain a fierce appreciation for the rule and practice of law, the multitude of avenues it can open for you and, more specifically, how it enhances people's lives.

Louisa Fitz-Gerald:

> *"Lawyers are the 'keepers of justice'. We provide the kind of help that people can't get anywhere else...I think we are in a unique position, in society, because we are able to help people."*

Brendan O'Brien:

> *"As lawyers, we get taught a lot about the way things work in society, and it's easy to take things for granted because of that education. If I ever deal with people who are either not*

particularly well educated or who have fallen on bad times, I am often reminded of how some people are completely oblivious to even basic administrative processes and because of that are often unable access basic social services. That's why law is important. Lawyers need to be able to explain in a way that's understood the way things work and what people's rights are, in order to genuinely help others in society."

Paul Redmond:

"...law is all about power, it's about distributing power and holding power to account by reference to law and to societal values, in particular to the value that everyone is equal before the law, the law applies to everybody equally, that we should be governed by law, not by men, that's a very fundamental value. It's often corrupted, but it's something that I think depends upon lawyers as agents for justice and agents for the rule of law. That's an enormous social interest. Lawyers have the capacity to do good because they understand how power works, the levers of power, and possess the tools of advocacy and effective representation."

Lucinda Clarke:

"Law maintains the civilised society that we live in. Therefore, lawyers should be treated with respect because of their knowledge and expertise. Why? Well, because these skills allow people to lead their lives how they want, just as long as they do not harm others. The rule of law, in my mind, is one of the greatest hallmarks of a truly civilised society."

Graeme Cowan:

"I think everyone should learn how a lawyer thinks, not from the point of view of if I need to be a lawyer, but it's a process for thinking and working out how to rationalise an argument. There are many other areas where that sort of approach can be applied apart from traditional law firms. I think there's a good number of parliamentarian sort of lawyers, a good number of merchant banker sort of lawyers, and so I think it's having a broader view of just working in a law firm because by the very

nature, it'll only be whatever it is, the top 50 per cent that will find a role in the law firms. But that doesn't mean that your skills and knowledge for law have been wasted, it just means I think you need to take a broader view of the possibilities."

How lawyers can effect meaningful change

"Tess" sums up the importance of law in a succinct and effective way.

> *"I suppose the healthier we are, the better results we will receive."*

This is applicable in any professional context that you consider. Comparatively speaking, the results I achieve when I am healthy and at peak wellbeing far surpass those in periods where my health and happiness is lagging. "Grace" came to a similar conclusion, which is that positive results flow when you take good care of yourself, and those around you.

> *"I don't think that society will necessarily fall apart if some lawyers have depression, because even though some people are unhealthy or unhappy, they can still be brilliant lawyers. But I do think that the legal profession, and society in general, benefits if everyone takes good care of themselves."*

This can also be applicable to the personal side of your life. Wouldn't you want to aid the people in your life whom you love to the best of your ability?

When my health was at its worst in mid-2012, I could barely get out of bed on some days. If a friend called me asking for help, I would have been in no position to assist in a meaningful, practical manner. I couldn't help myself, and thus had no chance of being able to help somebody else. Nowadays, I am consistently energised, driven and focused;

not only can I take charge of my own existence, but my friends and family feel confident in my ability to step up if I am needed.

Marie Jepson identified the commercial benefits that are associated with ensuring the health and wellbeing of yourself and those around you. According to Marie, you can put yourself in a much better position to achieve favourable outcomes for your clients if you are on top of your game.

> *"I think with perspective and balance, you perform better, you are happier, and you contribute more positively to your own work environment. In fact, it seems, to me, to be a 'win-win' situation for the organisation. And, truth be told, psychologically healthy people are better for business. You work better with your clients; therefore, you have a better relationship with them. You also work better with your workmates, so it is truly a 'win-win' situation."*

"Elizabeth", however, mirrored my own motivation for continuing my exploration into the law field, and undertaking this book project.

> *"The idea that I am going to be helping people is the real reason I'm still here."*

The consensus seems to be that the best way to combat the devastating effects of psychological distress, depression and/or anxiety is to focus on your own health and wellbeing first and foremost, so that you can make a tangible difference to those around you.

TWD Wellbeing Wisdom

In March 2011, Sir Gerard Brennan spoke at the launch of the UTS Brennan Justice and Leadership Program, a voluntary extracurricular program bearing his name that I helped establish when I was a law student. He articulated the importance of law and lawyers in our society in a manner so striking that it is now ingrained in my mind.

> *"A lawyer may be well regarded, and rightly so, as a pillar of society, belonging to the mainstream of social opinion, or as a notable contributor to his or her field of endeavour. Lawyers are charged with the responsibility of maintaining the rule of law in the community. If lawyers discharge their responsibility, their natural role is leadership. They know the infrastructure of our society, they are concerned about justice and freedom; they have the skills to articulate the causes of injustice and to alert the community to the need for remedial action. And by their uncompromising professionalism, they demonstrate the independence of mind essential to true leadership."*[51]

It has been four years since I sat in the front row of a lecture hall captivated by the oratorical eloquence of a person who once held the highest judicial position in the nation. I was overwhelmed with legal afflatus and left the room with a greater appreciation for the place of law in today's society. As Sir Gerard pointed out, legal professionals play a significant role in deciphering how and why our society operates the way it does. They are also responsible for shaping future societies.

By no means does this observation exude conceit or self-interest, although it would be naïve to assume that the legal profession does not occasionally come across that way to

51 Sir Gerard Brennan, "Launch" (Speech delivered at UTS Brennan Justice and Leadership Program Launch, University of Technology, Sydney, 17 March 2011)

"outsiders" or, in some cases, seasoned law professionals. It is simply to say that law students and young lawyers must be aware of the importance of their chosen vocation, and the underlying purpose for which the legal profession was born – to serve the community. The manner in which one enters a law degree program, and then, the legal profession, as was discussed earlier in this book, matters little when speaking in these terms.

Retention of this sense of service has the capacity, in my opinion, to provide fulfilment and satisfaction beyond what one could achieve without it. Removal of any feelings of disenchantment with studying and/or practising law, or even concerns surrounding one's emotional or mental wellbeing, can be sought through adherence to the idea that we, as law students, lawyers and legal professionals, are charged with the duty of combating injustice whenever and wherever we see it. We are also responsible for ensuring justice for all persons in our society.

Law permeates so much of our lives. As a community of select individuals, who have a better understanding than most for how the law operates, it is our ultimate duty to serve. Law students and young lawyers need to establish a positive professional identity that affirms the importance of being custodians in society. As a lawyer, you are responsible for being an agent of the law. In other words, your duty is to promote social order and justice.[52] This identity not only has a positive impact on sociocultural attitudes, within the law field, it also reduces psychological distress, anxiety and depression among legal professionals.

It is important to remember the following points:

- Law is an altruistic profession. It not only helps others, it also helps improve your own health and wellbeing.

52 Watson and Field, n 10, 395–6.

- You have skills, knowledge, and expertise that most people do not have, so use your talents wisely.
- If you can, draw inspiration from the services you provide to others. Use this inspiration as a means to overcome your psychological distress, depression and/or anxiety.
- In order to be the best legal professional you can be, you must first take a holistic approach to managing your health and wellbeing. This gives you the greatest chance of achieving your potential.

This is supported by the findings of Krieger and Sheldon, who surmised the following:

> *"...The tendency of law students and young lawyers to place prestige or financial concerns before their desires to make a difference or serve the good of others will undermine their ongoing happiness in life."*[53]

53 Krieger and Sheldon, n 2.

Resources: I need help. What can I do, where can I go, who can I turn to?

It is possible for the level of psychological distress, anxiety, and depression to become debilitating to the point where there is no choice but to seek assistance from a qualified mental health professional (i.e. counsellor, psychologist, psychotherapist, clinical social worker, or psychiatrist).

There is no shame in asking for help!

As you know by now, I had to ask for help. After my health problems came to the fore, I decided quickly to seek as much guidance from mentors, loved ones, and health professionals as I could. But for a period of approximately six months, I was resistant to the idea of taking anti-depressant medication.

I viewed this as some kind of surrender to the illness, or thought that I could tackle the illness by myself.

I was wrong on both fronts.

I struggled with medication in the initial stages, as it took me a few weeks to find a drug that was suitable for my physiological needs. But once I did, the pills had a significant calming effect upon me, just as my GP, Paul, had promised. What I found once I was settled into the routine of taking the medication was that not only did it stabilise my moods and keep me on track, but it also provided some security for me, in the sense that I felt I had a safety net to protect me from my own fears. This was, ultimately, a world away from those early terrors that I would somehow succumb to the illness… instead, it gave me another weapon with which to fight.

Often, legal professionals tend to believe that given their supposed above-average intelligence, competitive drives and pragmatic approach to life, they can manage every issue that they face. Unfortunately that is not always the case. I learned this lesson the hard way.

It is okay to accept help. Sometimes help is exactly what we need in order to get better. If utilising valuable resources helps you get back on your feet so that you can refocus your attention on achieving your goals, then why not seek as much relevant assistance as possible?

Listed in this chapter are a variety of helpful resources that you can explore, not just for tips of how to manage your health and wellbeing, but also how to proactively assume a holistic approach to your personal and professional existence, by caring for every facet of your being.

Websites/blogs

As a young legal professional, you may find that accessing these kinds of materials will be an easier hurdle to overcome than liaising with a depression hotline or health professional.

These sites provide anecdotes, experiences and articles from your peers so that you may better undertake your journey through law, and appreciate what others may be going through.

- Lawyers with Depression (**lawyerswithdepression.com**)

  Run by a partner in a New York law firm, Dan, Lawyers with Depression is a blog that provides a significant quantum of stories, guest articles, solutions and resources for managing depression within law. In addition, *LWD* provides testing modes to measure your levels of stress and anxiety.

- Survive Law (**survivelaw.com**)

  Survive Law is a leading online community forum for Australian law students and graduates. This forum offers articles and blog posts, and provides tips and guidance on every situation that law students and graduates may face as a young legal professional (i.e. from dieting during exam period all the way to the management of wellbeing issues).

- Beyond Law (**beyondlaw.com.au**)

  Beyond Law is a new resource for law students and graduates who are seeking employment in a range of professional fields. It takes into account the varying passions and interests of legal professionals. This can have the indirect result of improving wellbeing for young legal professionals by helping them access available opportunities.

- Lawyered! (**lawyeredforlawstudents.blogspot.com.au**)

  This website is run by a former university medallist (and friend of mine). It features a career blog that offers study/job tips, methods, and strategies that can help law students do their best, while in law school. Lawyered! is truly a fantastic tool, especially if the individual is unsure how to ace job assessments and/or make job applications stand out from the crowd!

- Oats and Sugar (**oatsandsugar.com**)

  This is the number one stop for UTS law students seeking high quality study notes. It is run by a former UTS business/law student (and friend of mine). Oats and Sugar features a blog that provides exam materials, personal insights on life as a lawyer, and presents volunteer opportunities. These invaluable resources help students and young lawyers apply for and snag their dream jobs.

- Graeme Cowan – I am Back from the Brink (**iambackfromthebrink.com**)

  Graeme Cowan is a former corporate bigwig who suffered with depression for years. He also attempted suicide on multiple occasions. Graeme Cowan is now an international author and public speaker, known for empowering people and helping them overcome depression. In addition to his website and books, he also has material available on YouTube and Facebook.

- Danny Baker – Depression is not Destiny (**depressionisnotdestiny.org**)

  Danny Baker "crowd funds" to cover counselling and therapy costs for those who cannot afford it. These funds are used to increase community mental health awareness. This website also features an extensive blog detailing Danny Baker's experiences managing depression. In addition, it provides readers with access to his books and articles.

Organisations and networks

These organisations and charities are so inspirational to me. I love their work and I love the people that represent them (at least those whom I have met) for their passion, dedication and motivation to help others in need.

- Tristan Jepson Memorial Foundation (**tjmf.org.au**)

  This leading charitable organisation helps raise awareness about mental illness. It also fosters positive practices in regards to depression in the legal industry. It was founded by Marie and George Jepson following the tragic suicide of their son, Tristan Jepson (a young lawyer) at the age of 26 in October 2004.

- Wellness Network for Law (**wellnessforlaw.com**)

  The Wellness Network for Law is a community of legal academics, practitioners and students who seek to address the high levels of psychological distress within the law field. The goal is to promote wellness in law schools, legal academies and legal professions. The Wellness Network for Law develops effective coping and management strategies that can prevent and/or ameliorate distress, and foster wellbeing within law schools and the legal professions. The Wellness Network for Law hosts a Wellness for Law Conference every year. This event is great for law students and young lawyers, because it teaches them valuable tips on how best to manage their wellbeing, and the wellbeing of those around them.

- Australian Law Students' Association (ALSA) (**alsa.net.au**)

  ALSA is the national representative body for law students around Australia. In addition to facilitating competitions for mooting, witness examination and other legal skills, producing educational and vocational publications and championing social justice issues in the law, ALSA also takes a strong advocacy stance in regards to mental health issues in law. Their website (and social media platforms) have a bounty of resources and written materials about how best to foster resilience for yourself and those around you in law.

- *Lawyers Weekly* (**lawyersweekly.com.au**)

  Lawyers Weekly is a leading news resource for all Australian legal matters. In addition, this website often features articles about lawyers who have overcome depression. Moreover, links to resources are available for those in the legal profession.

- Batyr (**batyr.com.au**)

  Batyr is a youth-based, charitable organisation that aims to empower young people by removing the stigmas surrounding mental health issues like depression, eating disorders, and alcohol abuse, among many others. Batyr normalises these issues by addressing the proverbial elephant in the room and by encouraging active participation in the reduction of health problems.

- Reach Out (**au.reachout.com**)

  Reach Out is a youth-based mental health service that provides 24/7 phone crisis services, 365 days a year. Reach Out offers assistance to youths suffering from a wide range of physical and mental health issues. This service is offered online because young people typically look for help online and thus is a valuable resource for those who seek assistance.

- Headspace **(headspace.org.au)**

  Headspace is a government-funded organisation that provides mental health counselling, education, employment, and alcohol and drug abuse assistance to Australian youths. The Headspace website also provides a significant range of online and downloadable resources that cater to an individual's personal needs.

- Mental Health First Aid **(mhfa.com.au)**

  Mental Health First Aid is an organisation that provides help to those who suffer from mental health problems, and those who are in the midst of a mental health crisis. It is a temporary solution until the appropriate professional treatment is received, or the crisis is resolved. Mental Health First Aid also provides evidence-based training programs which are authored by Mental Health First Aid (MHFA) Australia and conducted by accredited MHFA instructors.

Charities and depression hotlines

In the event that you feel the need, or see a friend or colleague who could benefit from an immediate conversation with a professional, you should keep this information handy.

It could save a life.

- Lifeline for Lawyers **(1800 085 062)**

  Lifeline for Lawyers was launched in June 2014 and is run by the Law Society of New South Wales. It is a 24-hour telephone support service for lawyers and legal professionals dealing with depression, suicidal tendencies, and/or other psychological issues.

- The National Institute of Mental Health (**nimh.nih.gov/index.shtml**)

  The National Institute of Mental Health is a government-hosted platform that offers information on depression, and other mental illnesses. The National Institute of Mental Health website also provides a bevy of downloadable materials, including a search engine for resources geographically close to the individual.

- Beyond Blue (**beyondblue.org.au**)

  Beyond Blue is an organisation that offers online and telephone assistance to almost 350,000 Australians. The goal of this group is to help people from all sectors of society. It focuses on public health initiatives and individual services.

- Black Dog Institute (**blackdoginstitute.org.au**)

  Many people are familiar with the animated video of a large black dog following people around. The Black Dog Institute provides great multimedia educational programs on depression and other psychological illnesses. In addition, it provides a wealth of effective treatment strategies for those suffering from psychological distress. Self-help tests and downloadable materials are also available on the Black Dog Institute website.

- SANE Australia (**sane.org**)

  SANE is an organisation that conducts innovative programs and campaigns to improve the lives of people living with mental illness. It also provides a helpline and website, both of which contain thousands of contacts from around Australia.

- Suicide Call Back Service (**suicidecallbackservice.org.au**)

  Suicide Call Back Service is a 24-hour telephone service available to people, over the age of 15, who are experiencing suicidal tendencies and/or are at immediate risk of suicide. This service is especially helpful for people in remote or regional areas.

Initiatives founded by lawyers

This kind of stuff makes me so proud to be a legal professional. If ever you get the chance to get involved with such initiatives, I strongly recommend that you do so – they will expose you to a whole new environment and culture within law that you may not have known previously!

- Bottled Snail Productions **(bottledsnail.com)**

  Bottled Snail Productions is a not-for-profit production company based in Melbourne. It provides legal professionals with an outlet to explore their creativity through performances (i.e. acting). The goal of this company is to fundraise for charities. In fact, it has raised over $40,000 for charities like TJMF. In addition, it attempts to teach legal professionals how to give back to their communities.

Justice Virginia Bell of the High Court of Australia's keynote address at the TJMF Annual Lecture in 2014 praised Bottled Snail Productions:

> *"Bottled Snail Productions is a proud sponsor of tonight's lecture, a circumstance that Tristan with his comedic talent would have thought fitting. Lawyers within the Bottled Snail set their management targets in a number of 'creative hours' worked. It is an idea that may be worthy of wider consideration.*

I await with interest the arrival of Bottled Snail Productions in Canberra."[54]

- Melbourne Lawyers' Orchestra (Lawchestra) **(facebook.com/Melbourne.Lawyers.Orchestra)**

  The "Lawchestra" as it is affectionately known is a not-for-profit group that is supported by Bottled Snail. This organisation aims to reduce the mental health problems in the legal profession through music.

Marie Jepson gives Melbourne Lawyers' Orchestra a glowing recommendation:

> *"...What they are doing is providing an opportunity for the creative side of people, within the law, to explore and do things along with their practices, and they're getting really positive responses. They're very reasonable in that they understand that law students can't come to every practice, but a lot of students are incredibly creative, and that has quite often, well almost, been drowned out of them, just not quite, you know, drowned out, well, beaten out of them, in the sense that they don't have opportunities, and they don't get the chance to use their talents. So they are using music as a proactive way to engage with other people, but also to develop their own passions."*

54 Justice Virginia Bell, "Putting the Guidelines to Work" (Speech delivered at Tristan Jepson Memorial Foundation Annual Lecture, Federal Court of Australia, 27 October 2014) <http://www.tjmf.org.au/2014/10/video-2014-tristan-jepson-memorial-foundation-annual-lecture/>

TWD Wellbeing Wisdom

There is not necessarily a right or wrong answer when it comes to seeking help for your health problems. But there are a couple of things I would recommend to you:

- Be open to suggestions from all trusted sources. Why? Well, because even an outlandish idea may hold the key that unlocks the mystery solution to your struggles!
- Remember that people who help you do it out of the kindness of their hearts. In other words, do not dismiss or ignore people who are genuinely trying to help you.
- Try not to expect to be miraculously cured overnight…these things can take time!
- Also, don't assume that by taking steps towards recovery, your problems will automatically be solved…it is not a matter of checking off boxes! There is a greater spiritual commitment to managing your wellbeing that you need to address.
- Make sure that you take the time to reflect on the progress you are making. Keep a diary, debrief with a friend, colleague, or confidant, meditate, or pray…whatever works for you.
- Lastly, it is important to acknowledge how far you have come.

So congratulate yourself on taking steps in the right direction. Asking for help is not an easy thing to do; but it is something that you will never regret doing!

Jerome's Story, Part II: Where am I now?

It's been almost four years now since my breakdown at the Falls Festival. It would be overly ambitious and indeed naïvely earnest for me to proclaim that I am completely out of the woods, or simply put – cured. Depression is not, in my opinion, an illness that is remedied in the same way as the flu. It is an ongoing process of management, care and support, so be prepared to do whatever you need to do to maintain your health, whether it be through counselling, medication, etc.

What I can say, with unbridled confidence, is that I now feel infinitely better. I do my best to not take anything for granted. I am extraordinarily grateful for the love, care and support my friends and family showed me during my darkest times. I truly believe that I would not be here today without them.

And while they would all likely say that I owe them nothing, I feel like I owe them everything.

I have resolved to show those people just how appreciative I am, and how much they mean to me. No amount of time, gestures, or kindness on my part will ever repay the debt that I owe them, but even as I make this attempt, I feel like it is one of the most important things that I will ever do in my life.

Armed with newfound emotional and psychological stability, as well as a strengthened resolve, I have been afforded a newfound appreciation for the law. It is altogether too easy for an outsider to dismiss the legal profession as a ruthless, overly competitive industry that exists to protect corporate interests. There are without doubt certain lawyers who fulfil these criteria; however the law is, and can be, so much more than this.

Legal professionals play a significant role in deciphering how and why our society operates the way it does. They are also responsible for shaping future societies. By no means does this observation exude conceit or self-interest, although it would be naïve to assume that the legal profession does not occasionally come across that way to "outsiders" or, in some cases, seasoned law professionals. It is simply to say that law students and young lawyers must be aware of the importance of their chosen vocation, and the underlying purpose for which the legal profession was born – to serve the community. The manner in which one enters a law degree program, and then the legal profession, as was discussed earlier in this book, matters little when speaking in these terms.

Retention of this sense of service has the capacity, in my opinion, to provide fulfilment and satisfaction beyond what one could achieve without it. Removal of any feelings of disenchantment with studying and/or practising law, or even concerns surrounding one's emotional or mental wellbeing, can be sought through adherence to the idea that we, as law students, lawyers and legal professionals, are charged with the duty of combating injustice whenever and wherever we see it. We are also responsible for ensuring justice for all persons in our society.

Law permeates so much of our lives. As a community of select individuals who have a better understanding than most for how the law operates, it is our ultimate duty to serve.

This book has discussed the importance of law in our society, drawing on the thoughts of interviewees. These thoughts centred on the horrors that could be, and often are, inflicted upon lawyers and law students who suffer from depression. If being a member of the legal profession can, in some cases, make you more susceptible to psychological distress, anxiety and depression, then it is also possible for one's membership in that profession to trigger enlightenment and courage as one identifies his or her place in the professional world.

I know it can, because that is how I feel about moving forward with my own professional career. I am a qualified lawyer with a relative quantum of skills and smarts. And I now know that it is in my self-interest to put my competencies to practical use in a field that not only matters to me, but will also matter to someone else. I mentioned previously that I would never wish my experience of depression on anyone else, and I meant that with all of my heart and soul. Fortunately, I am in a privileged position that affords me a perspective on the legal, educational, and vocational fields that is perhaps not as apparent to others. As a result, I feel that I can provide a beneficial service to the legal community and the community as a whole.

I am extremely motivated and excited about the future. I hope that the stories in this book help students and lawyers persevere through the dark times. Even if this book helps just one person, I will consider that a success.

Acknowledgements

I've always loved writing. Whether it be creative stories, research essays, personal letters or the cringeworthy poetry of teenage dreaming, there is something about expressing myself by putting pen to paper – as opposed to verbalising my innermost thoughts and feelings in an inscrutable fashion – that provides not only a great deal of personal comfort, but yields power and influence that I don't often feel with spoken communication.

That said, the production of this book has ultimately been a team effort; without the input, advice and support of a great many people, this project would never have come into fruition, regardless of any literary impulses I possess and practise.

But before I acknowledge those who helped me complete the book, I'd be remiss if I didn't preface that by thanking those people whose love saved me from my depression in the first place. To my parents, Ted and Nas – the debt I owe goes far beyond keeping me afloat financially in times where I was unable to find or even undertake work, and in the months where I wanted to focus solely on completing this book. The comfort and security I have been able to draw from your unwavering support, love and pride in me has been monumental. To my siblings, Oliver and Isabel, who have found ways over the past few years to look out for me despite being cities or even countries apart. In me, you have an older brother who will, in turn, always look out for you. To my closest friends, who were always there to guide me through the darkest of times as well as the minutia…Angus, Michael, Codie, Jack, Nicole, Lucy, Nushi, Kate O, Dan, Luke, Pat M, Edward, Talah, Heidi, Emily, Isha, Natalie and Alice – your friendship means the world to me. To my ex-girlfriend, whom I won't name, for the self-belief and confidence you were able to instil in me when I was a broken shell of a man – let alone boyfriend. To other friends who went above and beyond in ways that I couldn't ever ask or expect of them… Leslie, Claire, Ian, Caity, Geoffrey, Mitch, Will D, Emma, Sam, Ben, the other Will D, Aaron, Lisa, Nick B, Pat D, Mick, Mark, Claudia K, Claudia C, Kate T, Jess, Abby, Skye and Sophie…and probably others whom I've forgotten to list (but definitely haven't forgotten in my heart). To my mentors, Paul, Graeme, Terry, Maxine, Jill, Nick E and Laurine – you helped me see the big picture and re-navigate my personal and professional lives. To my medical professionals, Paul and Anna – you managed and navigated my health in ways that I found most comforting, especially when I didn't even want to seek help.

Without all of these people, the book would never have happened. Without them, I might not even be here today. Thankfully, though, I am still here. Because of that, I was able to put this book together. But I couldn't have done it without the help of some extraordinary professionals, both inside and outside of the legal field.

To Sir Gerard Brennan – you supported this project from

the outset when it was merely a concept bouncing around my brain. The support you offered, by being willing to lend your name to the project, instilled great confidence and motivation in me to not only complete the book, but do it to a standard that could hopefully make you proud. To Dr Robert Fisher, the enlightening and supportive psychiatrist who provided enriching perspectives as a medical professional – you have given this book more credibility than I could ever hope to bring to it myself. To Graeme Cowan, who provided the initial inspiration for this project and starting the writing process, by reinforcing my motivation to find a tangible, altruistic way to help others and therefore find catharsis in my own situation. To my entire family, who supported the project from the outset, especially my grandmother, Harriet, who funded the project in its entirety. To all of my friends, whose consistent enthusiasm and excitement for every trivial update I gave on the book – you made me feel like what I was doing was important, which pushed me to keep going. To my American freelancers, Kimberley and Ree, who completed extraordinary hours of audio transcription and editing respectively – you helped give shape to the entire project that I otherwise would not have been able to create. To my old mate George Pappas and his staff at G-Squared Digital Marketing – you created a fantastic series of online platforms for me, including the website and social media pages; I feel strongly that these mediums will garner success for the book that I otherwise could not have gotten. To my brilliant illustrator, Sammy Moore – I had a vision of what I wanted the book to look like, and you took that vision to new heights. With your talent, we've been able to put together a book on depression in law that is fun, fresh, edgy and inspirational. To Rod and Jon, the publishers at Xoum – your patience, diligence, hospitality, punctuality and professionalism have been so greatly appreciated. The book is so much better for having had your input.

And finally to you, the reader. Thank you for taking the time to read this book. I truly hope that it has been informative and useful. I want nothing but the best for you with regards to your health and wellbeing. If you have any questions following your completion of this book, please feel free to contact me via my website. I am here for you.

Select bibliography

Australian Law Students' Association, *Mental Health Supplement* <www.alsa.net.au/images/2011/2011_ALSA_Mental_Health.pdf>

Australian Medical Students' Association (AMSA) and New Zealand Medical Students' Association (NZMSA), "*Keeping your Grass Greener*" <http://mentalhealth.amsa.org.au/wp-content/uploads/2014/08/KYGGWebVersion.pdf>

Colin James and Jenny Finlay-Jones, "I Will Survive: Strategies for Improving Lawyers' Workplace Satisfaction" (2007), 15(1) *Legal Education Digest* 32 <http://papers.ssrn.com/sol3/papers.cfm?abstract_id=2320353>

Connie J.A. Beck, Bruce D. Sales and G. Andrew H. Benjamin, "Lawyer Distress: Alcohol-related problems and other psychological concerns among a sample of practising lawyers" (1995–1996) 10 *Journal of Law and Health*

Dr Norman J. Kelk, Dr Georgina M. Luscombe, Dr Sharon Medlow and Professor Ian B. Hickie, *Courting the Blues: Attitudes towards depression in Australian law students and lawyers*, (2009) BMRI Monograph 2009–1, Sydney: Brain & Mind Research Institute <http://www.cald.asn.au/docs/Law%20Report%20Website%20version%204%20May%2009.pdf>

Dr Sharon Medlow, Dr Norman J. Kelk and Professor Ian B. Hickie, "Depression and the Law: Experiences of Australian Barristers and Solicitors" (2011) 33 *Sydney Law Review*

Graeme Cowan, "The Elephant in the Boardroom: Getting Mentally Fit for Work" (Executive Summary), (2013)

Joel Orenstein, "The mindful lawyer meditation and the practice of law" (2011) 85 (7) *Law Institute Journal*

John Brogden, "Leading Change in the Legal Profession" ,(Speech delivered at the Tristan Jepson Memorial Foundation Annual Lecture 2013, Federal Court of Australia, 17 October 2013) <http://www.tjmf.org.au/2013/12/video-2013-tristan-jepson-memorial-foundation-annual-lecture/>

Joshua Wolf Shenk, *Lincoln's Melancholy*: *How depression challenged a president and fuelled his greatness* (Houghton Mifflin Co, 2005)

Justice Shane Marshall, "Depression: an issue in the study of law", (Speech delivered at the Wellness Forum for Law Annual Conference 2015, The Australian National University, 6 February 2015) <http://www.fedcourt.gov.au/__data/assets/pdf_file/0004/26608/Marshall-J-201502.pdf>

Justice Virginia Bell, "Putting the Guidelines to Work" ,(Speech delivered at the Tristan Jepson Memorial Foundation Annual Lecture, Federal Court of Australia, 27 October 2014) <http://www.tjmf.org.au/2014/10/video-2014-tristan-jepson-memorial-foundation-annual-lecture/>

Kath Hall, Molly Townes O'Brien and Stephen Tang, "Developing a Professional Identity in Law School: A View from Australia", (2010) 4 *Phoenix Law Review*

Lawrence S. Krieger, "What we're not telling law students, and lawyers, that they really need to know: some thoughts-in-action towards revitalising the profession from its roots", (1998) 13 *Journal of Law and Health*

Lawrence S. Krieger and Kennon M. Sheldon, "What Makes Lawyers Happy?: A Data-Driven Prescription to Redefine Professional Success", (2015) 83 (2) *George Washington Law Review*

Leanne Mezrani, "It is the worst time in living history to be a law graduate" *Lawyers Weekly* (online), 27 August 2013 <http://www.lawyersweekly.com.au/news/14603-It-is-the-worst-time-in-living-history-to-be-a-law>

Leanne Mezrani, "Lawyers Need More Time To Do Their Job", *Lawyers Weekly* (online) 19 February 2015 <http://www.lawyersweekly.com.au/news/16186-lawyers-need-more-time-to-do-their-job?utm_source=lawyersweekly&utm_campaign=lawyersweekly_Bulletin19_02_2015&utm_medium=email>

Leanne Mezrani, "You don't really give a damn about our mental health", *Lawyers Weekly* (online), 20 January 2015 <http://www.lawyersweekly.com.au/news/16068-you-don-t-really-give-a-damn-about-our-mental-health>

Martin E.P. Seligman, Paul R. Verkuil and Terry H. Kang, "Why Lawyers are Unhappy", (2005) 10 (1) *Cardozo Law Review*

Massimiliano Tani and Prue Vines, "Law Students' Attitudes to Education: Pointers to Depression in the Legal Academy and Profession?" (2009) *Legal Education Review*

Matthew Ball, "Legal Education and the 'Idealistic Student':

Using Foucault to unpack the critical legal narrative", (2010) 36 (2) *Monash University Law Review*

Michael Sandel, *Justice: What's the right thing to do?* (Penguin Books Ltd, 2009)

Molly Townes O'Brien, Stephen Tang and Kath Hall, "Changing our Thinking", (2011) 21 (1/2) *Legal Education Review*

Patrick J. Schiltz, "On Being a Happy, Healthy and Ethical Member of an Unhappy, Unhealthy and Unethical Profession", (1999) 52 *Vanderbilt Law Review*

Paula Baron and Judith Allen, "Buttercup goes to law school: Student wellbeing in stressed law schools", (2004) 29 (6) *Alternative Law Journal*

Prue E. Vines, "Working Towards the Resilient Lawyer: Early Law School Strategies", (Research Paper No. 30, University of New South Wales, 2 July 2011)

Sally Kift, Jill Cowley, Michelle Sanson and Penny Watson (eds) *Excellence and Innovation in Legal Education* (Federation Press, 2011)

Sir Gerard Brennan, "Keynote Address", (Speech delivered at UTS Brennan Justice and Leadership Program Awards Night 2013, University of Technology, Sydney, 26 September 2013)

Sir Gerard Brennan, "Launch", (Speech delivered at UTS Brennan Justice and Leadership Program Launch, University of Technology, Sydney, 17 March 2011)

Todd Peterson and Elizabeth Waters Peterson, "Stemming the Tide of Law Student Depression: What Law Schools Need to Learn from the Science of Positive Psychology", (2008) 9 (2) *Yale Journal of Health Policy, Law and Ethics*